A Beginner's Guide

To

Owning A Mule

A Beginner's Guide

To

Owning A Mule

Becky Coffield

MOONLIGHT MESA
ASSOCIATES

WICKENBURG, AZ

A Beginner's Guide to Owning a Mule

All Rights Reserved. ©2018 by Becky Coffield

Printed in the United States of America

Published by:

Moonlight Mesa Associates, Inc.
Wickenburg, AZ

www.moonlightmesaassociates.com

Printed in the United States of America

ISBN: 978-1-938628-29-0

LCCN: 2017918199

Cover design by Vin Libassi
Cover photo by Tom Coffield
Back cover photo by Debbie Humphreys

All photos by Becky Coffield unless otherwise noted

Dedicated to

Bouquet and Reba

INTRODUCTION

Beware Mule Fever!

Hold your horses, there! The frenzy, excitement, and utter lack of self-control and discipline that most people exhibit when it comes to buying their first mule is extraordinary. One would think that mules will soon be extinct, or that the first mule a person sees is perfect and there will never be another. When mule fever hits it can feel absolutely impossible to control, but controlling that frantic, exuberant urge may be the best thing you ever do for yourself.

Buying any equine should not be an impulsive decision, and that most definitely goes for mules as well as horses, maybe more so. It all too often is, however. A person gets an idea, they get excited, and they make a decision they might not have made had they taken more time, given it more thought, and done more research. Before one even starts looking for an equine, or in this case we'll focus on mules, it's important to ask yourself, honestly, the deep down reason why you want this kind of animal. Do you want a mule because your friends ride mules? Or because you love those big, brown, soulful eyes and beautiful ears? Maybe you want to be different than everyone else? Or do you want one because mules seem to be popular nowadays? Maybe you've simply heard intriguing things about these animals, or you rode a perfect one at the Grand Canyon or similar place. None of these reasons is necessarily bad (although it's clearly easy to spot a weak one or two), but once the newness of having the animal wears off and reality – sometimes a very harsh reality – creeps in, you may not be so enthused about your decision.

I think this is a very important question a person needs to answer before taking the plunge into "muledom." You should know upfront that mules are either loved or abhorred in the equine world. Those who have mules who have hit it off with them wouldn't trade their mules for any number of horses, but not everyone is this lucky. There are as many ghastly tales of mules and their owners as there are of horses – likely more. Many horsemen do not like mules at all and refuse to ride behind, in front, or anywhere near a mule, insisting their horse doesn't like mules. (Mule owners claim it's really just ear envy on the part of the horse.) Sometimes mules are not allowed to participate in competitive activities – largely because mules can do exceptionally well and often out-perform horses. And, while it's true that a mule can handle steep, rough terrain usually better than a horse, a good trail horse can handle this kind of terrain probably as comfortably as a mule.

The beginner mule owner often fails to appreciate that a mule is NOT a horse. Some mules are far superior to their equine relatives, a few are not. One big "problem" with mules is that they are extremely intelligent and are reputed to "think" for themselves. A mule is not for the simple-minded, impatient, or timid. A mule takes study, patience, and good riding ability, that's certain. You simply have to be smarter than the mule. Some owners aren't, or they're impatient and have problems as a consequence.

There are some who are attracted to mules because these animals are very much part of the history and fabric of America. Our first president, George Washington, is said to have introduced the mule to this country after the King of Spain presented Washington with the gift of a large jack that made a breeding tour of the south. Later Washington received yet another young jack, this time from the Marquis of Lafayette. This young guy seemed to be quite proficient at producing good saddle mules!

Mules have been used in almost every war this country has engaged in, with perhaps the exception of the war in S.E. Asia. (I could find no record of this, anyway.) In any event, the mule's history in the formation of this country is indeed profound. But that fact alone is not a very good reason to buy a mule.

From the outset, I believe in what author John Hauer calls "The Natural Superiority of Mules" – that mules have a vigor common in many hybrids. However, a mule is just not for everyone, and your reason for buying a mule, along with your abilities, temperament and determination can have a bearing on your success with this animal.

What I am going to present in this book is largely opinion – my opinion – much of which is based on my "mulish" experience. I am not a mule trainer or a "mule whisperer." I'm not a brilliant, accomplished rider. Even after several years of owning and riding a mule, I still consider myself a beginner when it comes to this incredible animal. Being a beginner, however, I'm very cognizant of beginner issues and snags, unlike folks who've had mules for years who likely have forgotten many of the pitfalls that beginners face. I have made many mistakes and run into many snags, believe me. In fact, I still do.

This book is not intended to discourage anyone from owning a mule, but I will tell you things that a person selling a mule might overlook or think not important. I'll offer some friendly advice on mule matters, and of course you're free to take it or not. Let me repeat: I am not a trainer or an expert. I am one who has had "mule fever" and made decisions I might not have made had I taken more time or the information presented here into consideration.

If you've owned horses, you probably have a slight advantage in this matter. In fact, I don't think a person should start their riding career on a mule. Many people agree with this, but there are just as many who think it doesn't really matter. I just believe a person should have some abilities on a horse first because a mule will promptly figure out if you're an inexperienced rider and very well might take advantage of you. Does this apply to everyone and every mule? Maybe.

There are people who started riding mules as a child because that's what the family owned. These are the lucky ones. And even if you're an accomplished horse-back rider, don't think for one minute that good horsemen make good mule-men. Again, don't make the mistake of thinking the animals are the same. Equally important, though, is that if you've owned a horse you likely know that equines need an owner who is on top of issues and behaviors before they become problems. A beginner often wants to treat their mule like a big pet. Mules are not big pets or dogs. They are large, powerful animals who can cause serious, or deadly, injuries.

Finally, I want to add that when you and your mule have fully "bonded" and you've grown to love the affection your mule bestows on you, there is just nothing quite like it. There's something unique and special about "mule love."

Once you have given serious thought as to why owning a mule is so important, you're satisfied that wanting one is not just a whim or impulse, and you feel you can care for it properly, you're almost set to start looking. My goal is to give you some suggestions to help you in your search and to help make your early days with your mule a success.

Reach deep into your wallet and buy a decent mule.—

Robert Fitterman, *WAR*, the musical

1. Buying Your Mule

So how does one select a good mule? Please, don't go out and start your search immediately. And whatever you do, please do not buy a green-broke mule in an effort to save money, especially if you are new to "muledom." Please. Instead, begin your search by learning *everything* you can about mules. It's ideal if you can go to a mule clinic. I know what you may be thinking: You really don't want to spend the money or the time to do this. After all, you might have to travel a fair distance and probably stay in a motel and eat in restaurants. It can be expensive, I agree. But let me assure you, spending this money and your time in this way is far cheaper than a trip to the emergency room after you've been tossed off the Floozy-mule you found on a website. Much cheaper. And the fact is you'll get more than your money's worth in knowledge if you can go to a reputable event where a *bona fide* mule trainer will be the presenter.

You don't have to own a mule to attend these clinics. You can go as an observer. Be sure to verify that the person conducting the clinic you'll be attending is a *bona fide* trainer, however, and not some weekend, self-made wonder.

I'd already bought my first mule, Bouquet (aka Bucket), before I went to Mule Days in Bishop, California, where I attended training sessions offered by Jerry Tindall. Oh! Did I ever discover how ignorant I was about mules! I'd ridden horses for a bit more than twenty years, but after just one of Jerry's sessions I felt absolutely flummoxed when it came to sweet little Bucket.

So, read about mules, try to attend a clinic or two, go on a mule ride(s) if possible, and talk to mule people – lots of mule people. A clinic or an event like Mule Days in Bishop or elsewhere is a terrific way to meet mule-people and learn. Mule events are held literally all over the country. I strongly suggest you not develop mule fever and buy a mule at one of these events, however, until you are *very* confident in what you're doing. Also, don't avoid talking to the people who abhor the critters either. You can find out more about why mules can be "so godawful" from people who don't like them than from people who love them and can't praise them enough. It's difficult to do this – it's akin to hearing people say negative (but possibly true) things about your children. You likely don't want this kind of information, but it's important to take it into consideration. Oftentimes a person parts with a mule on bad terms because the animal was poorly trained or badly treated by a previous owner, or sometimes the person was just not temperamentally suited to own a mule – or had an ill-fitting saddle (more about tack later) that caused the mule to buck or misbehave. The mule may have physical problems that have never been addressed. Maybe, just maybe, the seller was misled by the previous owner or mule broker.

Facebook has many groups you can join to find out about mules, ask questions, and *possibly* even find mules for sale. This is not at all intended as an endorsement of those sites.

As mentioned previously, the best book I've ever read on mules is probably John Hauer's *The Natural Superiority of Mules*. I myself prefer the first edition because of the photos and artwork, but the second edition is likely more helpful for beginners. It was John's book that put the final touches on my decision to buy a mule instead of another horse. Of course the book has its slant because John is a fantastic mule-man!

Once you've done some serious homework, you're much less likely to make an impulsive decision, so go ahead and begin your search. Don't rush.

For starters, I'd like to suggest that you be wary of people who say, "Oh, anyone can ride this animal. Even our grandkids are safe on ol' Floozy here." Here's the problem with this endorsement: usually the people who say these things are either a): excellent riders and could ride a bucking bronc without much concern and have forgotten what it's like to be a beginner; or b): they are trying to unload the mule for any number of reasons, many of which might be legitimate, but some of which could be hazardous to your health. And, just because the grandkids can ride the mule, doesn't mean you can! So, rule number one: Beware the mule that "anyone can ride." Maybe the mule *can* be ridden by anyone. Maybe not.

Rule number two: if they say "the animal is doing well under saddle," be wary and read that to mean "the animal hasn't been ridden much and is pretty green!"

Perhaps you have a friend who is willing to sell you a mule. That can be either very good, or the end of a friendship, so think about this carefully. In my case, I bought my first mule from a friend. I was very perplexed because I couldn't figure out why she wanted to sell this darling little mule. I'll say that I was told upfront about the mule's "bad" habits, and one was that she was extremely difficult if not impossible to catch. The other issue was that the mule did not want her ears touched, likely because a wrangler at a big group ride apparently had "eared" the mule for some disciplinary reason. Never ear a mule – ever. She had a few other habits I learned about as we went along, but most of those issues resolved with time and patience, and also when I changed her tack.

I rode the mule before buying her and I could see she was more than a bit on the anxious side, but I was a bit nervous myself, so that didn't deter me from buying Bouquet (a.k.a. Bucket). I knew I could buy a snap-on bridle, so I wouldn't have to mess with her ears at all when bridling her. And I figured I'd find a solution to not being able to catch her – which I eventually did, by the way. However, there were a few other issues that arose as time passed, but ultimately things went extremely well for my little mule and me. So, the point of this is simple. Try to find out the *real* reason why your friend wants to sell the mule. Sometimes the reason for a sale is simply a matter of economics – it costs a lot of money to keep a mule (or horse). Other times the owner might concerned that the animal isn't being ridden enough. There can be many valid reasons for selling the mule, so don't shy away. I'm so glad I bought Bucket. That little mule taught me a lot, and your mule will teach you a lot also – hopefully only good things! I'm not advising you to turn your friend's mule down, but definitely ride the mule a few times and see how things go before making a decision. A friend will not (*should not*) purposefully mislead you.

If you buy a mule from a person who makes their living buying and selling mules, make certain the person is reputable. You will need to do a little sleuthing perhaps, but I have a friend (we'll call her Gail) who bought a mule that was advertised on Facebook. Gail, a truly engaging person but a bit impulsive, didn't do her homework and didn't know the seller had a shady reputation. As a result, the mule almost killed her. Besides the horrible injuries she suffered, she also lost her confidence in riding which, once lost, often never really fully comes back. In Gail's case, the seller sent a video showing the mule doing marvelous things, so Gail didn't feel she needed to take the time to actually go and see the animal (only 4 hours away). Please. If you absolutely must buy the mule this way, at the very least make certain there is a return clause. Any reputable seller should be willing to refund your money or replace the mule with another if you have problems! In fact, *anybody* selling a mule should be willing to do this. Gail found out after the fact that the seller wanted no part of that idea. (More about Gail and her misadventures later.)

It's also very possible that the person selling the mule truly believes the mule is bomb-proof and completely safe. However, if you are relocating the mule to a new environment, you probably should be prepared for a few "issues" to arise until the mule is settled. I purchased my second mule, Reba, in Missouri and transported her to Arizona – two *entirely* different environments. I bought Reba from a mule handler who praised Reba's many attributes. However, having had one mule already, I suspected some issues might arise because of moving her to a totally new setting with a multitude of changes including a new rider, and I was right. So make sure you give your mule a chance to adjust to all the "newness" before you panic and call it quits.

Sometimes you may be so blessed as to be given a mule. My husband Tom was, and what a terrific animal! Tom wasn't even sure he wanted another equine after the horse that he'd ridden for 27 years died, but he is now attached to his john mule, and he'd be loath to part with him. Not everyone gives away a "perfect" mule. What we discovered is that the behaviors the mule sometimes did that disappointed the previous owner, he never did with my husband. Don't count on being this lucky, however.

Some people like the idea of adopting a mule doomed to the slaughter house or one that has been abandoned. These are noble ideas. I myself have adopted many rescue dogs and not been disappointed, but a mule is not a dog. Buying or adopting a rescue animal is a book unto itself. You may have no problems and only eternal gratitude from the animal, or you could end up with a pasture pet or worse, a nightmare. This is probably not a good idea for a new mule person.

Try very hard to contain your excitement about buying a mule and don't buy one sight unseen. Your life might depend on this. I know what you may be thinking – there she goes again: gas to buy and maybe a motel and terrible restaurant food to pay for, but let me repeat - these expenditures are a small price to pay compared to a trip to the emergency room and months, even years, of pain and agony. Hitting the ground from any height can do permanent damage to a body, so keep that in mind. Does this mean you'll be running around the countryside spending your mule-money on travel? No, not if you've familiarized yourself with mules by attending a clinic, reading all that you can, and talking with people. However, once you have decided on a mule, I believe wholeheartedly that you should see the mule in person, watch it, and ride it before you fork over your hard-earned money and haul it home or have it delivered.

I also would like to suggest that you avoid buying a very young mule. Mules live a long time and can be ridden well into "old age" if kept active and healthy, so buying one that's around the age of 10 or older is not a problem. The issue here is that most people really don't know, or accurately remember, the exact age of their mule. It's not like a child in that regard. The years pass and people tend to forget how old the mule was when they got him and how many years they've had him. I don't think anyone is trying to deceive a buyer. A breeder, however, would probably know a mule's exact age, and an equine dentist would be able to give a buyer a *very* close estimate.

When you start looking at prospective mules at clinics and other places, it's a good opportunity to start looking at conformation. This can be a difficult area for a beginner to judge. Most of us are not "conformation" experts, but it won't take long before you begin to notice things about the way mules are built. Some buyers may think conformation is not all that important – they just want a nice, safe animal, or they want a really "pretty" one. But bad conformation can potentially make riding more difficult and might even lead to future problems for the animal.

Try your best not to get enraptured with a mule's coloring or other external features. Do your best also to watch the mule's behaviors. Forget "pretty" and concentrate on behavior and disposition.

You'll soon notice that some mules are friendly and perhaps curious. Others are standoffish. Some may seem distrustful. I've heard many experts say that a mule's disposition is more important than any other factor. I think this is true, but as a beginner you'll likely have a hard time assessing the animal's overall disposition. Riding the animal may be a big help in that department.

I suggest that you have the owner *unsaddle* the mule if the mule is saddled when you arrive. You need to see the mule without gear on. The seller could be trying to hide "saddle sores" among other things. Then watch the seller re-saddle the mule. You'll get a good idea if the animal has ground manner issues. Plus you'll get to see where he places the saddle on the mule.

Once you've narrowed your search and are focusing on a specific animal, make a list of questions. It's easy to forget some if they aren't actually written down! And don't overlook some of the more "detail" things. For example: When were the mule's teeth last floated? Is the mule up-to-date on vaccinations, especially rabies and West Nile Virus? Some people don't vaccinate their mules. Obviously, we do. Their thinking is that mules are hardier than horses, so why do it? (Vaccinations are discussed in chapter 7.) When was the mule last wormed? Does the mule have a worming schedule? (Worming is discussed in chapter 7.) Has the mule ever been lame?

Has the mule ever colicked? Can the mule be ridden out by herself? What kind of bit has the mule been ridden with? You personally need to lift the mule's feet…all four of them. Your shoer is not going to like it very much if he has to fight for the feet. If the mule is already in a pen when you arrive, ask to have her turned loose to see if she can easily be caught. Watch her with the other animals – if there are any. Is he or she the alpha of the herd? Are you able to be the alpha to this animal? Or does it look like the mule is at the bottom of the pecking order?

In addition, *you* need to load her into the trailer – or at least *a* trailer – to see if she loads easily. Not the seller. YOU. If you've traveled very far, likely you'll be stopping for the night. Will you be able to load her again in the morning? Some mules don't like being by themselves in a trailer, either. We were *extremely* pleased that Reba loaded every single morning on our trip back from Missouri. I did put our dog in the stud stall by her during our driving time, hoping his companionship would keep her from being too lonely. And at every fuel stop I went into the trailer to give her a cookie and to reassure her. It probably wasn't necessary for her, but it was for me!

Reba is an exception about loading and riding in the trailer alone. My husband's mule can be a major handful and then some if trying to load him into a trailer by himself. And once I hauled Bucket to a ride by herself and she was a trembling, sweaty wreck when I unloaded her. It took that little girl an hour to calm down. When you go to buy your mule, you might consider taking another equine along in case your new mule balks at being trailered solo. Ask the seller about this. Often sellers suggest that the mule be transported by a professional hauler – maybe now you know why.

You need to ride the mule, and not just in a pen. Ask the owner to saddle up and go with you as he will likely give you suggestions for handling the mule better. In my case, I'd never really used my legs much with my horse when giving "directions," and my mule had been trained to respond to leg cues. (And I'm still trying to remember to do this more!) But this is good to know. Does the mule neck rein? Plow rein? Or both?

Before you take off with your animal, a vet check is highly recommended, but not always practical. A vet can verify if the mule is in good health. A farrier is another person I wouldn't hesitate to talk with. Farriers know feet far better than vets. You don't want to have to put special shoes on your mule or worry about all manner of foot ailments that you don't know about. When I bought my first horse I had the vet come and check him out. The only correction she made to the owner's description was that *if this horse is four-years-old, he just turned four.* That should have told me that the horse was still pretty green, but since I was a green rider it went right by me. A farrier, however, could easily have pointed out how poor the horse's feet were for his size. I owned that horse for over twenty years. I grew used to him tip-toeing over rocks, tripping regularly when he loped, and finally needing pads on his feet. Would I have bought him had I known all these things? Probably – because I fell in love at first sight. Try not to do that.

What kind of feed has the mule been given? This question may seem obvious: of course, mules eat hay. But there's all kinds of hay, and some may not be appropriate for a mule. Most mule owners advise against giving a mule straight alfalfa unless the mule is a genuine working animal. It's thought to be too rich for the animal (in fact it's too rich for many horses too). Many mule owners don't believe in giving their animals grain of any kind…again, too rich. Remember that the mule is part donkey, and free roaming donkeys eat brush, shrubbery, and all manner of weeds and other items. They don't dine on grains and rich pasture grass. There's nothing wrong at all with giving your mule good orchard grass, timothy grass or even Bermuda, but probably not straight alfalfa. We feed our mules rye with just a touch of alfalfa. However, when feeding any grass, you might want to be careful how much you feed your animal until you know it better. You don't want an obese mule, and some are easy keepers – just like some people! So, find out what kind of hay and how much the seller feeds. Try to get something similar if at all possible. Does he open feed? Twice a day feed? Is the mule on pasture? Maybe it's a combination of feeds. You should probably know this. You may have to help your mule adjust, slowly, to a new feeding schedule and new feed in general. Our seller sent home five bales of hay from his field to help Reba make the transition from his feed to ours in Arizona.

The soil in our part of Arizona can be sandy. Even though we put the animals' feed in containers, sometimes a lot of it ends up on the ground. My husband's mule likes to throw his around and eat off the ground, in fact. So monthly we give the animals psyllium for a week. This helps remove sand from their digestive track and hopefully helps prevent colic. Depending on your mule's environment, you may not need to do this, but some veterinarians advise that this should be done at least monthly for all equines who are in a dirt/sandy environment. Some animals eat off the ground and never pick up any sand; others are not so dainty. Feed is expensive, so try to feed your mule in such a manner that it won't get thrown on the ground and walked on.

Now, you'll notice the price of mules varies greatly…so do hotel rooms. And just like staying at a Ritz

Carlton or a Motel 6, you pretty much get what you pay for when it comes to mules, sad to say. Can you buy a cheap mule that's any good? *Yes, you can.* You can get lucky. Of course an experienced mule buyer can judge a mule easier than a novice, which is why some people hire a "professional" to look for a mule for them. I myself have never done this, but I know people who do. Sometimes they're very satisfied; sometimes not so much. I think part of the "fun" of owning a mule is the shopping, although I will admit that when a person is hungry to own a mule taking all that time searching may seem tedious. If you remember that your life can be at stake, however, it's not so tedious after all, is it?

Why do mules tend to be so expensive? That's a good question that has many possible answers. One thought is that it takes a mule longer to mature than a horse, so the training time is delayed and the breeder must keep the animal around longer, feeding and caring for it before the animal can be trained and sold. There's an urban (or maybe country) legend that mules quickly become bored with repetition, so the training must be more sophisticated as far as how much time is spent on an activity and the number of different activities offered to keep the animal interested. I'm not sure about this one.

And because mules cannot reproduce (or very rarely) that likely puts a bit of a damper on them being over-populated.

Are mules more dangerous than horses? No, not really, but that's hard to say as a certainty. Ideally a person should spend this much time buying any equine. But mules are stronger (pound for pound) and often faster than many horses. Fortunately, I think they also tend to be calmer and less flighty. Probably what is the most troublesome thing about mules for most people is that they "think" for themselves and are highly concerned with their own preservation. Mules are just not for everyone.

Since I've owned mules, I have repeatedly seen people buy a mule they've never taken the time to go and see for themselves. Some of these animals are doomed because they are more trouble than the inexperienced buyer can handle or even knows how to handle. The last time I saw this happen the mule turned out to be a kicker. You don't want a mule that kicks! That dangerous habit was omitted by the seller when he spoke to the buyer on the phone. Even when a person goes and sees the mule and does all the things I suggest, things can still turn out badly.

Which is better: a john mule or a molly? Everyone has their opinion on this. I have owned two molly mules and my husband owns a john. Most all of the other mule riders I know own molly mules. I think johns tend to be bigger and thus stronger, and maybe not quite as willing to cooperate when they don't want to. They do have character though! And even though mollies do most of the performance activities, johns are very capable. A friend rode her john mule in a 25-mile endurance race and won. In the 50-mile race, though, her mule quit just a short distance from the finish line. He refused to be budged or bribed into going further. Nope. He was finished. A horse will run itself to death – not a mule. So, molly or john? Your call, but ask a lot of people who've ridden both what they think.

Finally, if you've paid a great deal for your mule, you might want to think about insuring your animal. It's not expensive compared to having to walk away with nothing but a memory. I paid a lot of money for Reba. My policy on her is $300 a year…that's less than $30 a month. That covers death from colic and theft, etc. Mules don't colic, you say? Yes, they do. That's how my first little mule died.

A stupid mule is still smarter than a good horse or a bad man.

Ursula Vernon, *The Tomato Thief*

2. Making Friends

What's she talking about now? Making friends with a mule? *The mule is an animal. It can't be a "friend"* – is this what you think? Most mule owners will not agree with you. However, I've learned the hard way that friendship does not mean you are equals! Someone has to be in charge, and if it's not you, I guarantee you that your mule will take over.

When you bring your mule home, or he/she is delivered, it's a good idea to give your new friend some time to settle in and adjust before you saddle up and ride off into the sunset or go on a group ride. Because Bucket was a bit of a pill, I actually spent the first two – almost three – months just interacting with her on the ground. I would visit her large corral multiple times a day. For the first several weeks she would run off. Instead of chasing after her and trying to catch her (which I tried several times much to her utter delight) which is never successful with mules, I learned to turn my back to her and offer my husband's horse in the adjoining corral some treats. It seems that mules do not like it when you turn your back to them. Every single time I'd do this, she would quickly and quietly come up behind me and stand with her nose about two inches from my back. I learned after this experience to use psychology on her – when I could come up with something.

Sometimes I'd take a chair into the corral in the evenings and sit and play my harmonica (probably more alarming to her than calming) or I'd read the newspaper aloud. Mostly she kept her distance and acted like she was ignoring these activities, but I could tell she was watching. After a few weeks, however, she stopped running off when I'd enter her corral and she'd allow me to approach within her neck-stretching area to offer her a treat. She could stretch that neck longer than a giraffe's. More time passed and she no longer ran from me at all and would let me ever-so-slowly approach to give her a treat and gingerly stroke her out-stretched neck.

Eventually I set up portable fence panels when I fed Bucket so I could enclose her. This allowed me to get into the enclosure with her and pet her to my heart's content. It also gave me the chance to halter her up if I wanted to ride that day. At first she grew extremely tense and nervous when I'd enter her pen and halter her. I'd always give her a cookie, though. It didn't take long and she stopped the nervous reaction and contentedly ate while I haltered her. And it was indeed a glorious day when I could finally walk up to her in the corral and halter her. It took about four months for this to happen. It took PATIENCE.

Your mule will most assuredly not take nearly as long as Bucket did to come around. With Reba, I saddled her up a few days after bringing her home. That was probably a bit soon, but she seemed relaxed and showed no signs whatsoever of avoiding me, running off, or otherwise misbehaving or being nervous, stressed, and afraid that I felt comfortable riding her after I sensed that she'd recovered adequately from the long trip from Missouri.

During this "getting you know you" period, it's a good time to order whatever bit the previous owner used on the mule. If the previous owner used a britchen, buy a britchen. If a crupper, buy a crupper. I don't think a person should try to start off on a new mule with tack the animal is not used to. An experienced rider may be able to do this without a problem, but even then I have my doubts.

Take this downtime to groom your mule as often as possible. Visit with your new animal before you turn in for the night. Feed your animal yourself. If your spouse normally feeds, make sure that you feed during this "getting to know you" time. Feeding your animal teaches it that it can depend on *you*. Halter your mule up and take it for walks on your property. Make sure all the gates on your property are closed, however, in case your new friend spooks at something she has never before seen and gets away from you. Remember, you may see a scampering rabbit, a bird flitting out of a tree, or a regular cow grazing contentedly, but your mule may see this:

(And just because your mule may have been raised around cows and is used to them, does not mean she won't react fearfully when she sees them in the wild.)

Talk to your mule the whole time you're working with her. Get her used to your voice. And when you take her for a stroll, wear gloves and do everything in your power to not let her jerk that lead line out of your hands if something startles her. If she does, she has just learned that she can escape from you at will.

You can do all these things and see no noticeable improvement in your mule's response to you. Don't get discouraged. Try to remember that mules seem to take their time to decide if they like you. You cannot rush a mule into anything, let alone rush it into liking you.

Of course, every mule will be different. I've owned two mules on the opposite end of the spectrum from each other. As much as I dearly loved Bucket, however, I have to admit that Reba is the easier mule. Is she perfect? Not at all, but she's darn good. She might be even better were I a better rider and more knowledgeable owner.

My friend Gail did none of the above. She spent at most a few days petting and visiting with her mule, which is all I did with Reba, but what made the difference? For one thing, I bought Reba from a well-known mule handler. I actually drove back to Missouri and rode the mule along with the seller; I handled the mule and I was with the seller when he handled the mule. For another, I'd owned a mule previously so I was not *quite* as green with mules as my friend. When Gail decided to ride the mule, she did not have the appropriate bit or a saddle that fit the mule correctly. She also allowed someone to walk up to the mule while she was mounted to adjust her stirrups. This alone may have been enough to set the animal off. As long as I'd owned Bucket, even she did not like having a person standing on each side of her – and she distinctly disliked having her tack adjusted when I was mounted. That was a red flag alert if ever there was one. Reba, on the other hand, is absolutely impervious to my readjusting her gear when I'm riding.

Many mules are said to not like fast movement from a handler and prefer people to move more slowly than they might with a horse. Quick movements can alarm them. This was quite true with Bucket – not so with Reba. So when Gail's husband approached the mule to adjust her stirrups, did he approach quickly? Likely he simply walked up in normal fashion – probably not a good idea with that mule. This is something Gail might have learned had she spent more time working with her animal before trying to ride her…something she might have learned had she gone and seen the animal, handled it, and ridden it before she bought it.

Making Friends

If you're going to trail ride, now would be a good time to see how your mule handles some trail issues. How does she handle the noise of a plastic water bottle? This seems simple enough, but it's not. Tara, an *excellent* rider, was riding her husband's new mule to "check her out" before her husband rode her. Not even thinking about it, Tara removed a plastic water bottle from her pommel bag and opened it. The unexpected crinkling set the mule in motion and Tara ended up on the ground. Even digging around in a pommel or saddle bag can unsettle an animal.

If you've brought your mule home to an entirely new area, this might be a good time to slowly test what she will do when she meets other animals on the trail. I have to say, Reba gets quite excited when horses appear. That mule loves horses! I myself am not terribly excited about her response, and this is something I do need to work on.

Depending on where you live there will likely be new experiences your mule will encounter on the trail. Now is a good time to introduce some of those if you can and try to desensitize her. Will you be riding with a dog, or will your partner have a dog along? This can be a major issue that will be covered in another chapter, but for now know that unless raised around dogs, mules often see these animals as predators and react accordingly. How does your mule react to children? Important to know! (The mule/dog issue is *extremely* important and will be discussed in chapter 4.)

Remember, it may take your mule a long time to warm up to you. Unlike a horse, a mule is not won over just because you feed her. Be patient and spend as much time as you can with your new charge, talking to her, grooming her, and petting and scratching her. Once she fully bonds with you, if she does, you'll know it. Bucket did not show any affection toward me until I left town for a few weeks and had to board her. When I returned, she let me know she'd missed me. She was definitely *my* mule after that. In her case, absence made the heart grow fonder. Reba, on the other hand, is an easier-going mule and has never been standoffish or aloof. I'm still not sure she "loves" me like Bucket did, but she likes me well enough. This could be because I've not spent the hundreds of hours with Reba that I spent with Bucket working through that little girl's peccadillos.

There are some who will scoff at these suggestions. It's your call, but I think it's only humane to spend time helping your new mule adjust. It's good for you too.

So, my suggestion is to take the time to make friends with your mule. You'll learn a great deal about her in the process, and she'll learn about you too.

In the world of mules there are no rules.

Ogden Nash

3. Tack

There may be as many opinions about tack as there are different saddle brands. However, this is an important topic. You simply should not expect to just slap any saddle on the back of a mule even though some people do…or try to.

As I'm sure you know, mules are built differently than horses. They often have very "mulish" withers (they take after the donkey) although some may have respectable withers. Some have flat backs, others are more rounded. In any event, a proper fitting saddle is a must when it comes to any equine.

You don't have to purchase a mule-saddle *per se*. There are many saddle-makers, but only a few who make saddles specifically for mules. Sometimes a western saddle will fit a mule just fine. My husband rides with his original western saddle. He has a good-sized john that has decent withers. My original saddle was too big for

Bucket, so I sold it and bought a saddle built for mules. The new saddle fit Bucket fine and works for Reba. (I took all my tack with me when I went to Missouri to buy Reba. I wanted to make sure my gear fit her.) Also, as an aside, I regret selling my original saddle. My advice is to never sell your tack…you never know when you may need that saddle again!

Finding a good-fitting saddle is tough because saddles are extremely expensive, so it's not like you can buy one and then easily return it to purchase a different one. When you buy your mule, see what kind of saddle the owner has been using. It helps if you have someone with you who knows good saddle fit when they see it, too. When you're researching mules, ask other mule riders what kind of saddles they use or recommend. If you're able to work with a saddle-maker, that's perfect. He or she will be able to tell you if your saddle is a good fit or not. A reputable person will not try to sell you a saddle you don't need.

A good mule-saddle should have sufficient hardware to enable you to change your rigging as you see fit. The saddle I ride in, built by Rick Ericksen (Ericksen Saddlery in Ennis, Montana) has great hardware. I found, after a number of rides, that I needed to have Reba's front cinch on the first ring and the back cinch on the first ring also. I was able to make these adjustments because of the fittings. You'll also need sturdy fittings on the back of the saddle to hook a crupper or britchen to (also spelled britchin, britching, breeching or any number of various renditions). Many saddles built for horses don't have these options.

Some people don't ride with a britchen or crupper. If you live where there isn't much terrain variation, you can no doubt do this. If, however, you live where there is any terrain at all, or plan to ride in an area with hills or mountains, you will definitely want a britchen or crupper. I recommend that you go with whatever the previous owner used. (If, by some bizarre chance the owner didn't use either item, don't expect to put a britchen or crupper on without the possibility of an unpleasant response from your animal. It may take a bit of time for her to become comfortable with the contraptions.)

Why is a britchen or crupper needed? You don't want that saddle sliding up onto your mule's neck when you go downhill. Remember, the mule does not have the same wither structure as a horse. If the saddle rides up on the mule's neck, I guarantee that you'll be in a precarious position. It's possible you'll only slide over the neck and onto the ground. Some mules will begin bucking. Both my mules tossed their heads and ran full steam downhill when that saddle pinched those withers. Personally, this is too much excitement for me.

Don't be surprised if it takes a spell before you get the britchen set just right, either. I learned through continuous trial and error. It can be very frustrating.

So, you have your saddle, a britchen or crupper, now what? I recommend a breast collar. Again, some mule riders don't use these as they don't think the saddle will slide back all that much – that mainly it just slides forward. I use one, but we often do some steep uphill travel. One time I tried riding without the breast collar. That was the last time too.

As for a saddle pad…I have several and it's best if you do have more than one. There are many styles and makes of saddle pads. These pads are expensive, so choose wisely. Picking one out is almost as time-consuming as shopping for new boots.

I started using a CSI saddle pad after I attended Mule Days in Bishop. It was a pad that my saddle-maker recommended. I also have a Tacky-too pad, and a 5-Star. Once I finally adjusted my britchen correctly, I no longer had trouble with my saddle sliding forward, and I found the CSI and 5-Star pad to be very good for staying put, although the Tacky-too pad stays extremely well also. The only problem with the Tacky-too is that it doesn't absorb moisture, so if you ride in warm or hot weather like we have here in Arizona or just about anywhere south of the 35th parallel in the summer, the sweat can be a problem. I use the Tacky-too more in the winter months, and I tend to rotate the pads.

I do like that the liner on the CSI pad is reversible. It attaches to the main shell with a velco strip, so it can still be used if one side of the wool liner becomes damp. It's a particularly good pad if your animal has developed "white spots" from nerve damage or irritation due to ill-fitting or improperly placed tack. Sometimes these areas can also occur because the equine may not be exactly the same on both sides, so no matter how good your saddle, problems can arise. The CSI pad will keep the area from hurting. If you ever have a chance to see a demonstration of these pads at an event, by all means do so. Also, the inner liner can be replaced, so you don't have to buy an entirely new pad when it only needs a new liner. The website for more information on this pad is www.csisaddlepads.com. (I have no financial stake or interest in this company.)

When it comes to bits, there's a plethora of them lining tack store walls. For starters, I would recommend that you use the same bit the former owner used with the mule. After several months with Reba, I changed her to a mechanical hackamore. I did this because she had the annoying habit of playing with the bit, shaking her head, and in general distracting herself and me with these antics. This, by the way, is not all that uncommon for mules to do. In addition, the seller had recommended I use a cotton cavasson to keep her from playing with the bit and also from grabbing food along the trail. By the time I put her rope halter on, the bridle on, and then tied the cotton cavasson on to help keep her mouth closed, I often felt exasperated, and it just didn't sit well with me having to "tie her mouth closed." After I deleted the cotton cavasson and changed her to a hackamore, she stopped shaking her head and she seemed much more relaxed. I will admit if I rode in an area where there were tasty morsels (bushes and sticks she liked) along the trail, I had to pay sharp attention and be constantly alert to keep her from dropping her head and grazing. The minute I dropped my guard, her head would go down.

I've been told that the hackamore doesn't have enough "whoa" power to stop a mule. I can only say that I think there are very few people who can actually stop a mule that runs away with them whether the animal is wearing a bit or a hackamore. A mule is unbelievably strong and has a powerful neck. Even a bit cannot stop a mule that isn't inclined to stop. It's very easy for the mule (or horse also for that matter) to clamp that bit between their jaws, stick their neck out, and just do as they please. The only issue with the hackamore is that a very strong person could, potentially, break bones in the animal's nose if too much pressure is applied. So, if you are a

Charles Atlas type, you might want to keep this in mind if you choose to use a hackamore. Because of her head shaking, the hackamore simply seemed to work better for Reba and me than a bit, although it did become irksome trying to keep her head up from grabbing at every blade of grass or bush we passed. And she didn't always respond as well in the hackamore as she had in a bit. After trying the hackamore for over a year, I reluctantly returned to a bit. Once her teeth were fixed, though, the head shaking and playing with the bit *completely, utterly, and absolutely ceased.* (More about teeth in another chapter.) Many mules, however, have the habit of messing with their bits. A lot of your decision regarding a bit will depend entirely on the mule. I have a few friends who ride their mules using a hackamore and have absolutely no problems whatsoever.

As far as a bridle goes, I use one that is a snap-on. I started using this because Bucket didn't want her ears touched, and when Reba came along I saw no reason to change.

Reba wears a rope halter when we're riding and I'm grooming her. She wears a break-away halter for travel in the trailer. *Never* turn your mule out with a halter on. If that halter becomes caught on any obstacle, no matter how small, the animal can die of suffocation as it struggles to get free. Remember, a mule cannot breathe through its mouth! It can only breathe through its nose, so if the passageway gets pinched off, that mule will slowly and painfully suffocate as it struggles for air. Always take the halter off before turning an animal out, even if turning out in a pen or corral. Please. I've been scolded about this in the past. After I saw a photo of a mule dying because the halter got caught on something, I *never* leave the halter on.

The photo (p. 34) shows a very small assortment of bits. The middle snaffle bit is a good bit for training. I never did take my quarter horse out of this bit. The twisted wire snaffle is said to be very "punitive" as you can imagine. However, once it's used, you may find the equine responds promptly and courteously with just the lightest touch. I rode Bucket with the top left bit, and I ride Reba with the top right bit. A person could get lost looking at bits, so try to use the one that the seller used or recommended, at least to start off with. Remember that the bit is a form of communication. It should *not* be a form of punishment. So if your mule does not behave the way you think she should, don't get a bigger, stronger, meaner-looking bit, which is what many riders do. Both you and your mule probably need some instruction and schooling to correct problems.

Ideally, a well-trained animal can be ridden with the "original" hackamore, not the "mechanical" hackamore which many people tend to use.

If you rode a horse before buying your mule, some of your tack items will likely work just fine on your new critter, like your breast collar, for example. Even your bridle can be adjusted to fit unless the mule's head is too big. However, it's a terrible idea to try to make the saddle fit by adding shims, extra padding, more blankets and the like. It's possible your western saddle may work out just fine, but be prepared that you may have to buy another saddle.

By far the best piece of advice I received when it came to saddling my mule was from the woman who sold me my CSI saddle pad. I had continuous trouble with Bucket shaking her head and running downhill. Very simply, if you find your mule inclined to do this, it's probably because you are putting the saddle too far forward. Remember, a mule's shoulders rotate differently than a horse's shoulders do. You don't want the saddle sliding onto those shoulders because it pinches the animal and is very painful.

I have come across two methods for saddling a mule. The first method puts the saddle pad itself just behind the withers. So, after putting the saddle pad on the mule, place the saddle two or three inches back on the pad. Put your hand under the saddle to make sure it is not on or too near the back of the scapula. Now, this may seem like the saddle is set too far back. In fact, one old-timer told me that if the saddle looks like it's set too far back, you have it in the right place. I'm not completely sold on the validity of his claim. Likely you will not follow this advice, so when your mule begins tossing her head and running downhill, or bucking, try setting your gear behind that scapula! Once I started setting Bucket's saddle like this and adjusted her britchen, all the head-tossing and running downhill completely stopped, almost like magic. I went through the same thing with Reba. I'm probably a slow learner. If I have that saddle set correctly, both my mule and I are much happier.

However, a good friend well acquainted with mules showed me another way to set the saddle. I often let this person ride Reba at a mule ride I organize while I stay in camp to greet people. He advises to place the pad forward, then the saddle is set so that **the bar** is behind the withers. If your britchen and other tack are set correctly and you are cinched up adequately, that saddle will stay in place. I'm not real great at getting the saddle always set correctly using this method. When you purchase your mule, make sure the seller shows you *exactly* where he sets that pad and saddle. It could save you a lot of time and exasperation. It seems like placing the saddle should be so simple – just put the dang thing up there. But for many mule riders, it's not.

A big issue regarding either method is to cinch up. The back cinch (aka girth) should be comfortably snug, or don't bother with it. (Remember, though, the mule needs to be able to breathe!) The forward cinch needs to be snug also. If the britchen and breast collar are set right, you don't have to fret about cinching up like it's a corset. However, I find I have to snug-up Reba several times when I'm saddling. Sometimes I think the cinch is secure, and when I go to check it, I can take up a good three or four inches more! She's quite proficient at holding air. Try to remember to cinch up in small increments. Don't just give a whopping big jerk on the old latigo. Your mule (even your horse) will become "cinchy" if you do that. It's a very mean thing to do, and very poor mulemanship.

Should you have your mule shod or not? Of course, as you probably know there's heated controversy over the shoeing vs. barefoot approach. Both sides have adamant advocates.

In the opinion of many, if your mule has always been shod, then keep her shod. Mules are known for strong, tough feet. However, they are not invincible. We ride in extremely rugged terrain, so I keep my mule shod. The one year I had Reba's shoes pulled for the summer to try the "natural barefoot" approach, I ended up having to buy very expensive boots for her front feet when we rode. The boots were great, but when fall came and we began riding longer, rougher trails as the weather cooled, I didn't want to take a chance of her going lame, so I had shoes put back on. She also developed thrush that summer, likely from standing barefoot in urine spots to cool her feet. (That's what I was told.)

If your mule has never worn shoes, depending on where you ride she can probably remain barefoot. However, if you are relocating her to rocky terrain it may be best if she is shod. And if you keep her barefoot, it doesn't mean you can skip on the farrier services. Those feet need to be kept trimmed and shaped regularly to prevent serious foot injury. Nothing is free about equines.

Keep your tack clean. Let me admit upfront that I'm a *fanatic* about this. Anyway, don't let your britchen or crupper get soiled with mule poop. The crupper especially should be wiped clean after every ride. Keep your girth clean. Have at least two. I prefer the combination mohair/cotton ones over the straight mohair or straight cotton. They are way more expensive than plain cotton, but they last much longer. These can be easily washed out in a sink and hung up to dry. I put ours in a pillowcase that I secure with a rubber band and wash them in the washing machine in cold water. The pillowcase keeps all the hair from clogging the machine! Don't use the dryer! Let them air dry. Don't let your cinches get all stiff with sweat and dirt either. That doesn't show pride of ownership. I doubt you'd wear dirty underwear, so don't make your mule ride with a stiff, sweaty, filthy girth. This advice, of course, is my personal opinion, and from what I've seen many people aren't as fussy as I am about the cleanliness of their mule's tack. I prefer the nylon straps over the leather because the nylon ones can be easily removed and thrown in the washing machine, again using cold water. Line dry.

As for reins, I ride with split reins. One problem with split reins is the chance of accidentally dropping one while riding. Oops. I've done this, of course. Hopefully your mule is well behaved and will "whoa" with a verbal command and maybe a small squeeze on the other rein so you can retrieve your dropped one! Another nice feature of the split rein is that you can use them to tie your animal when you stop for lunch. My reins have snap hooks that attach onto the shanks of the bit. I just unhook one of the reins, hook it onto the rope halter and then tie up. I also carry a lead line to use as an emergency rein or for tying up. Some people don't like the reins with the snaps on the end because they say they can get caught on brush. I suppose this can happen, but in over 20 years of riding horses and/or mules on all kinds of trails, it has never happened...yet.

My husband rides with a continuous rein. They're shorter than the split reins which is also a problem for my mule because she likes a loose rein! Some of this is controversial, to say the least. Just use what works and feels best to you.

A saddle bag is a good idea to have also. Some riders only use a pommel bag. A pommel bag is fine if you're just out for a short ride. If you ride two hours or more, however, I believe having a saddle bag is important. I dedicate one half of the bag to my mule with medical supplies, treats, spare rein, lead line, hoof pick, etc. The hoof pick comes in very handy if a rock gets caught in your mule's shoe. I also carry a comb because it's much easier to remove cactus spines from your mule (or yourself) with the comb than with your fingers. The other half of the saddle bag carries my items: tiny first aid kit, water, snacks, perhaps a lightweight rain jacket or sweatshirt, a compass in case I don't have replacement batteries for my GPS with me, matches, and things of this nature. My only *nonmedical* suggestion here is that if you are diabetic, you might want to consider carrying some insulin or appropriate food or snack. You never know what may happen on the trail or how long you may unexpectedly be out! Also, if you are allergic to bees, carry an Epi-pen. I also put any required permits in a zip lock bag and carry those in my saddle bag. In addition, make sure your saddlebags are evenly weighted. A lop-sided bag can actually pull your saddle off kilter if one side is much heavier than the other!

The new GPS I bought will actually work while inside a saddle bag now, so when I carry a water-bottle holding bag (like half a pommel bag) I have my GPS in one pocket and a cell phone in the other. Sometimes I ride with a small firearm on me. I admit that the fire arm sounds extreme. Where I live, it's really not.

Arizona does not require a concealed or open carry permit. I don't plan to shoot anyone, but there are other dangers in the desert (and forest, too, for that matter). Honestly, I would not want to fire a weapon off any equine not trained for that noise! Although my mule has been certified for search and rescue and has been exposed to gunfire, smoke, sirens, etc., shooting at something while mounted can be extremely risky. I'd have to be pretty desperate before I'd pull a trigger while on Reba. You may live in a lovely, predator-free area where this is not a concern. However, if for some reason I were to end up on foot in the middle of nowhere, having a weapon might save my life…assuming it's not in my saddlebag on my mule heading down the trail.

My friend carries some of these items (cell phone, water, etc.) in a fanny pack that goes around her waist. Her thinking is that if she falls off her horse and it takes off and these things are in the saddle bag, she won't be able to use them (like call for help). She wants the items on her. That makes excellent sense, but I carry so much stuff that using a waist/fanny pack would be impossible, and it's a lot hotter here in Arizona than where she lives in Oregon. I don't need extra things on, but having a cell phone on me is a very good idea.

I encourage you to order some "i.d. tags" for your mule, the kind sold for dogs work just fine. I have one on both my mule's halters and one on her bridle. If she ever gets away from me in a strange area, I'd like to think that the people who find her would return her if they knew how to contact me. Mules, like horses, are herd animals, though, and if your mule runs off when you're with other riders, it's likely she won't go too far. Keep some treats handy to entice her back or that will allow you to approach her. If she ran off, however, something probably scared her and now she may have lost some confidence in your ability to keep her safe. Most animals can find their way home if they're in a familiar area.

I came across a great item not long ago – you might be familiar with it. It's called a "cool vest." There are all kinds of these. Some have gel packs, some just use water. I bought one that I put into cold water for ten or fifteen seconds, then I gently squeeze the excess water out and put it on. It is a great device if you ride in really hot areas. If the water evaporates, just dip it in a stream or water trough and start all over again.

As for spurs…a spur with short rowels will likely suffice. You will not need some two-inch+ long rowels. The benefit of the spur is that for some people it's easier to give leg cues. Don't forcibly jab spurs into the mule's side…that's not their purpose. If your mule hasn't been ridden with spurs, tread lightly. Spurs can cause serious, unpleasant, even deadly reactions from a mule (or horse) when worn by an inexperienced spur-wearer! Learn to use your spurs sparingly – if at all. Always remember that they are used for communication, not punishment.

As far as helmets go, I've only recently started to wear one. They're a good idea and can be cleverly decorated into a "hel-hat." When I lived in Oregon, almost everyone wore a helmet. In Arizona, I see very few people in helmets. Maybe the heat discourages people from wearing them, or it's the "cowboy" image they prefer. At my last mule ride, I saw a woman's helmet after she was thrown from her animal...had she not been wearing the helmet, her head absolutely would have been cracked open.

My "hel-hat" is pictured below. You can find easy directions on how to make your own "hel-hat" on various websites. Here's one: https://www.facebook.com/media/set/?set=oa.12814596 48537254&type=1.

Note the bucking rolls on the saddle pommel. I attached these because my saddle is too big for me. These do help keep me a bit more secure should I get tossed around a tad.

Note the ample sized rings on the back of the saddle used for attaching the britchen or crupper.

I have been an author for 20 years and an ass for 55.

Mark Twain

4. Time to Saddle Up

If you're new or somewhat new to this equine business, saddling up may take a bit of time at first. Even after many years of riding, I still take more time than my husband. Don't rush. Get it right. In addition, you may have a mule that doesn't like people moving quickly around it.

For the beginner, by now you've undoubtedly spent a wad of money at the local tack store buying grooming tools. My opinion? Always groom your animal before saddling up. Brushing (currying) your mule will remove any items, however small, that could lie where the saddle pad or girth fit and then could rub on her causing a sore. It doesn't take much to cause a sore, even a teensy piece of twig can cause injury. Check your pad also before placing it on the mule's back. Make sure that tiny bush parts, etc. are brushed off. If you've been a rider, this is not news.

If your mule's tail is knotted up due to the previous owner not tending to it, don't hack that tail off. It will become untangled with patient combing! Don't try to get it all untangled in one attempt. Take your time. Use a spray like ShowSheen to help with the detangling.

In the process of saddling up, it's a good idea to check your mule's feet to make sure that no rocks or pebbles have gotten embedded in the hoofs. Not everyone does this because their animal may be kept where there's no ground debris of this kind. I'm ashamed to admit that I don't always check my mule's feet before I take off (although usually I do) and that's actually not a good thing to omit. However, I *always* check her feet and clean them upon return. If you don't check them before you leave, though, your mule could have a rock wedged in her shoe which could cause her to develop a very sore foot and even go lame.

Make sure the britchen or crupper is adjusted correctly. Not too tight or the britchen will rub raw spots on the mule and saw the hair off. It's not at all helpful if it's too loose, however, and a loose britchen can allow the saddle to slide forward onto the mule's neck if going downhill! You want to be able to put maybe two fingers at most under the britchen where it comes down over her hip bone. Ideally the saddle shouldn't move more than an inch, maybe two, either way. Once you get the britchen set and feel it's correct, you shouldn't have to readjust it any more. One idea is to not cinch up until you have the britchen in place and checked that it's a good fit. This saves you from having to cinch up, then uncinch and move the saddle, then re-cinch, etc. If you're very strong, you can just leave your britchen (and breast collar) attached to saddle. I don't need this extra weight to hoist onto my mule's back.

Be gentle with your animal's ears when putting on the headstall. And don't shove the bit into your mule's mouth. Make sure the bit is on top of the tongue! There are a lot of sites on the web that can help you adjust your bridle if you don't know how and need help. Or have a friend help (as long as you're sure they know what they're doing.)

You should be able to mount your mule while standing on the ground. If you can't, perhaps you should ask yourself why you've selected such a tall mule. What happens if you need to mount up out on the trail and there's nothing nearby to stand on, like a fence or rock? Face it, if you're a *new* rider I'm pretty willing to wager that you will probably fall off at least once. It's not a matter of IF you fall off your mule; it's a matter of WHEN. *Even expert riders take spills.* This happens, especially with new animals that you're unfamiliar with. You'll probably not get hurt other than a sore behind. It's embarrassing, shocking, and often frightening. Now if you can't mount back up because you have Goliath for a mule, it's maddening.

Even if you can mount from a standing position on the ground, it's a good idea if you have a mounting block or platform to mount your mule, especially if you're a bigger person. When you put that foot in the stirrup and pull yourself up onto that animal's back, there's a tremendous amount of torque on that back. Out on the trail, look for a log or rock to stand on. Your mule won't stay still while you try to mount? Now you have something to work on!

Early on, check to see that you can mount and dismount on the opposite side of the mule from what you normally mount and dismount on. I think this is actually quite important to be able to do. The first time you try mounting from the opposite side, you might have a friend stand by the side of the mule and hold onto a rein...just in case! Once I dropped my GPS when we were on an incredibly steep hillside. It was a long slide down off that mule. When I finally found the ground which was much further down than I thought, my head was about even with the mule's belly. There was NO WAY I was going to be able to mount from that side. I was very glad I could mount from the high side! Periodically mount and dismount from the "wrong" side to keep your animal used to it. (And sometimes when I've saddled up, I'll see that my saddle may be a tiny bit "cock-eyed." Mounting on the opposite side of the "cock-eyed-ness" helps straighten it out.)

Before you go galloping off down the trail, many people recommend that you take a few minutes and warm your mule up by doing a few bending exercises using your leg and rein. This isn't mandatory, obviously, but it's a good thing to do. Do I do this? Rarely, but after a recent clinic I attended I guarantee I'll now do it more often. If you don't know how to do these simple exercises, the web has *many* sites you can reference, or a more experienced rider or teacher can show you. (Again, make sure any advice you get actually comes from knowledgeable people. And a knowledgeable mule person will not be rough or hurtful to the mule.)

When you return from your ride, check your tack as you take it off. After all, you've spent a lot of money on these items! New tack won't show any wear and tear probably for years to come, but as your tack ages, or if you have used tack, you'll want to check for potential problems. Should the nylon cinch straps be washed? Are any of the attachments or hardware showing wear? Wipe your saddle and gear down as you put it away. After all the tack is removed and put away, take the time to brush the mule out. Re-comb her tail if needed. Check those feet using a pick to remove debris and any small embedded rocks. Now's a good time to check for thrush, chipped hooves or, heaven forbid, missing shoes. I don't want to be sexist, but if you're a woman, you should be able to lift your mule's feet. What will happen if you're out on the trail and your animal picks up a rock in its hoof and no man is there to help remove it? If you can't pick up your animal's feet, this is something to work on. And many animals aren't very cooperative about this – but you would already know that had you taken the time to do this when you bought the mule.

If your mule returns crusted with sweat, you might want to rinse her off before putting her away unless it's cold. If you're unsure whether she likes this or not, start with just her feet and legs and slowly work your way up. If you're returning her to a dirt pen, you may want to leave her tied for a short spell so she can dry a bit. (I wouldn't advise rinsing them at all if it's quite cold, nor do you have to do it or need to do it every time.) In any event they'll roll regardless once they're turned loose. My mule loves her face washed after a ride. So be it. I wash her face and gently cool her down using a wet cloth on her head and around her ears. She almost purrs!

Don't forget to clean the britchen or crupper if your mule pooped along the trail. If you used a crupper, check to see that the area under your mule's tail isn't red and inflamed. Sometimes it takes an animal time to get "toughened" up back there, especially if they haven't been ridden much with a crupper on or it's been a long time. Next time you ride, you'll want to make sure the area is healed up, and double check to make sure you have the crupper adjusted correctly. If your mule has a red, scratched up area or an open sore under her tail, very gently clean the area, then use something like Neosporin on the wound. Your vet may have a better ointment in mind, but Neosporin is my go-to medication for dogs, equines, and myself! Don't use the crupper again until it's healed. Switch to a britchen.

Another thought…don't give your mule treats while saddling her. I promise you she will become an absolute nuisance in her search for treats in your pockets if you do so.

This "Tuff-Enuf" crupper is my favorite when I don't
use Reba's britchen. It's easy to adjust as you ride.

Here's Reba with her britchen. We often ride very steep terrain. I've been told that a crupper can cause back discomfort if riding steep terrain. I don't know if this is fact or fiction, though. I tend to alternate between the britchen and the crupper.

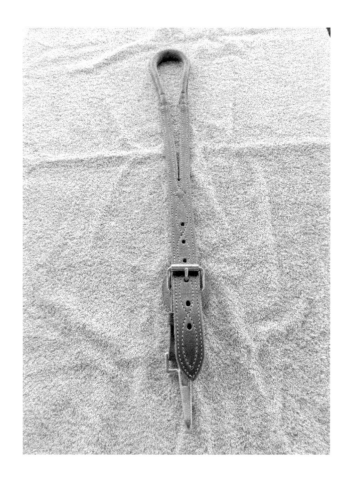

This is a beautiful crupper, but very stiff and difficult, if not impossible, to adjust while riding.

5. On the Trail

Not all equestrians trail ride, so this chapter may not be helpful if you intend on using your mule strictly for dressage, hunter/jumper, or any other kind of showmanship. Even if you plan to use your mule in this manner, however, all equines need a change of pace and a chance to get out periodically, so trail riding would be a very good thing to incorporate into your riding regimen.

Don't take trail riding for granted because "all your friends trail ride." Trail riding is actually one of the most dangerous activities you can do with an equine, especially when riding an animal that hasn't been ridden on the trail all that much, or maybe ever. There are *a lot*, and I do mean *a lot* of things on the trail that can frighten your mule. Even if you have a seasoned mule, if you are riding in a completely new area, your animal can be anxious, excited, out of sorts, and unpredictable. (This is something I know from experience, I regret to admit.) The more often you trailer to new areas, though, your mule should become more relaxed and not so much of a nervous-nelly.

Again, let me remind you that a mule is concerned with self-preservation, so you need to have a good seat, heels down, and be paying attention. Even a bird rushing out of a bush unexpectedly, or a rabbit darting from under a shrub, can scare the dickens out of any equine, mule or horse. And some animals are simply high strung and nervous by nature, so no matter how many miles they have on them, they too might easily startle. If it's windy be prepared that your mule may be more nervous than usual. She may be picking up on smells from far away that you can't detect. I myself don't much like riding in wind, but sometimes it arises when we're a long way from the barn!

As you mosey down the trail, there are several things that your mule may try to do that you should put a stop to. The first thing the animal may decide to try out are all the tasty bushes and shrubs along the way, the drier the better. Don't let your animal eat on the trail. It's a bad habit and it will get annoying when they are continuously lowering their head to grab a snack. It's also possible the animal can get into something poisonous. Some people do let their animals eat when they stop for a spell. I don't know if this is wise or not, but I'd say it's not.

When your mule stops and raises her head with ears alert, she likely has spotted something she is unsure of or smelled something that alarms her. Don't spur her in the ribs and urge her to go on until she has had a moment to check things out. You don't have to give her five minutes to sniff and stare, but give her perhaps 30 seconds or so and then gently urge her on. The more you ride, the less frequent these stops will likely be.

Keep a close eye on your mule's ears. They'll tell you a great deal. If they're flopping away, it means she's relaxed and all is well with the world. When they stand alert, you had better be alert also. Of course, when they get angry, those ears get laid back.

Another bad habit some equines develop is a tendency to want to speed up when they know they're headed home. Equines apparently have a great sense of direction because it doesn't take very many times at all riding out before the animal knows when it's headed back, even if you've trailered somewhere new and are heading to the trailer. Do not let your mule run back. If you want to move out faster for a spell, that's fine. But make sure that you bring your animal to a walk, and a walk at a pace of your choosing, the last quarter-mile before you are home. WALK HOME. NO RUNNING! Horses are actually worse than mules about this, I think.

Your mule can even find her way home if you think you're lost. It's embarrassing to admit, but once my friend and I got lost on BLM land not far from my house. We spent close to an hour looking for the road that took us home. We had no idea which direction was which because of the heavy shrubbery growth. (This was before the arrival of GPS.) Finally I decided to see if my mule could find the road. She immediately started walking with purpose, and in *less than 20 seconds* she located the road we'd been searching for. We just hadn't seen it because of weeds and sagebrush. So, if worse comes to worse, give your mule her head and she'll probably head back to the trailer or the barn without your guidance.

Besides imaginary monsters along the trail that your mule may see, there are some valid dangers. If you live in bear country, you'll likely know there's a serious predator in the vicinity by your mule's behavior. The same goes for mountain lions, bob cats and other creatures of this nature. Respect your mule's sense of smell, hearing, and vision. Will you encounter any of these predators? *Most likely never.* In all my years of riding in the Sisters Wilderness and adjacent areas, I had very few experiences where a mountain lion or bear was present. I only knew when they had been there because of the bloody animal carcass abandoned along the trail, and my horse's anxiety attack at the smell of blood…and cougar.

In my mind, one of the most terrifying experiences for animal and rider is an encounter with a deadly snake. (Well, maybe a bear would scare the willies out of me too.) If you're lucky, your equine will sense or smell the snake in time to avoid it. But not always. Interestingly, I have learned that if a mule (or horse) is struck in the face by a rattlesnake, supposedly their odds of survival are pretty good if they don't develop an infection, which is why it is *always* important to call a veterinarian as soon as possible.

If you're riding in snake country, it's wise to carry two short hose pieces, maybe 8 inches long, so that you can keep your animal's airway open. Have the bottoms of these two tubes connected in some manner so your mule doesn't snort them into her airway! You'll have to put these items in your mule's nose. Is this an easy thing to do? *Absolutely not.* But remember that your mule cannot breathe through her mouth, so if her airway swells closed (and it will if a snake strikes her in the face) she will suffocate. The swelling will be enormous, so don't even try to keep the bridle on. This is a good reason to ride with a rope halter on your animal. Keep the rope halter from becoming too tight, and slowly walk home or to your trailer. You most likely will not be able to ride because of your mule's condition. If you are in an area with cellular coverage, maybe someone can come and pick you up – or not. If you're able to place a call, have someone summon a vet so that they're ready when you arrive.

If your animal is struck in the leg, it seems her odds of survival are not so good. The problem is that the enormous amount of swelling cuts off circulation to the foot. Usually an equine cannot be saved because the foot doesn't last long without circulation. This is another reason why you must be very attentive when trail riding.

Now, not all areas have poisonous snakes, but many do. Reba was actually struck in the nose while on our property eating brush and sticks or whatever else she chooses to snack on. Did she see the snake? Probably not. Most equines will not stick their nose into a bush if the snake is rattling! Many can also smell snakes just as some people claim to be able to do. With Reba, I'm not sure what happened, or how. I just know I found her very shortly after the attack, probably within 15 minutes, maybe 30, judging by the amount of swelling. Already she had labored breathing. It was terrifying. Not to mention my final vet bill was over $500. I was happy to pay it, though, to save her life. After this experience, if we ever happen upon a snake on the trail, I suspect I'd better be ready for a strong reaction on her part! Mules do not forget! The only good thing that came out of this, besides my mule being alive and well, is that I became much more aware of the terrible consequences of being struck by a rattlesnake. I'd always been rather cavalier about not carrying a flashlight outside at night when checking on the animals, but when I saw how dramatically my thousand-pound mule's face swelled within minutes, I could only imagine how much worse the reaction would be on a person.

I also think bees can be a problem. You don't even need to be trail riding to get stung by a bee, but bee attacks seem to becoming more and more common. Despite an equine's size, they can dramatically over-react when stung by a tiny bee. I finally talked my doctor into giving me a prescription for an Epi-pen. He commented that he didn't know I was allergic to bees. I told him I wasn't, but that about the time my mule got stung, bucked me off and galloped away in a frenzy, and I was on the ground being stung a thousand times, I probably would be! I'm not sure the Epi-pen would even save a person were that to actually happen. And of course, my Epi-pen would most likely be in my saddle bag on my mule heading full speed down the mountain.

As you ride your new mount, you'll come across many items that may test your pucker factor – things your mule may be afraid of because she has never had experience with them before, or because she had a *bad* experience. Is she afraid to cross water? I bet you forgot to ask about that when you bought your mule! I asked my seller about that, and we walked across a dinky stream, but it was frozen over. (Reba doesn't really like crossing water, I found out. She'll do it, but she's not exactly eager.) Usually a mule or horse will follow others across water rather than be left behind alone. Do not dismount and try to lead the animal across. This is a good way to be seriously injured or even killed. Your mule can panic and leap forward, knocking you down and potentially killing you in the process. This happened to a rider not that long ago here in Arizona. When you go home, assuming your mule has not crossed the water, you can work on this problem by creating puddles, etc.

There is no way to predict what might scare one equine but not another, or what might frighten your mule one day but not the next. The key here is to do your very utmost to remain calm in situations where your mule is not at ease. And there will be no doubt in your mind when this occurs. It's *extremely* difficult, maybe impossible, to remain calm in the face of potential disaster when you feel that thousand-pound animal tense and that head comes up with ears alert! But if you don't remain calm, or at least in a semblance of control, your mule will sense your fear and will feed off it. You can count on that.

Unfortunately I know this first hand. To minimize your fear, and hers, try singing quietly, humming, or talking to her in a quiet, calm voice. Take some deep breaths. Let her stand for a minute or two and collect herself (while you collect yourself). Assure her that you're there to take care of her. Ultimately if you're very frightened, it may be best for you to avoid that situation for the time being and go a different direction. Don't allow this to happen very often, though, or your mule will learn to throw hissy-fits to avoid doing things she doesn't want to do. She won't forget!

A hot issue that frequently arises is dogs on the trail. Many equines are raised with dogs around and are not bothered by them. However, just as many do not like encounters with dogs, especially strange dogs. **Keep this in mind: you are legally and financially responsible for any injury to an equine and/or rider if your dog causes them to have an accident or injury.** You may have friends who ride with dogs, so make absolutely certain your mule is not bothered by their presence. A friend I enjoy riding with often takes her dog along. The dog is inclined to take off in one direction and return in another. If my mule does not see the animal approaching, I can have my own little rodeo when the dog crashes onto the scene. Remember that many mules, if not most, see dogs as predators, and the mule is, once again, all about self-preservation.

On one occasion I was riding with a friend who had two dogs accompanying her. We ran into mutual friends on the trail who had four dogs with them. Good grief. It looked like a kennel escape. An absolute melee ensued as the six dogs barked madly and ran wildly after each other among the horses and mules. Quite honestly, it was very unnerving to be sitting atop my mule as barking dogs cavorted and ran insanely wild.

Mules are also not keen on dogs following too close behind them, even if they are mules that are used to dogs. Keep in mind that mules can see their hind feet, so they know when a dog is at hand.

It goes without saying that if you ride during hunting season wear red, and it's best just to stay out of the area! For some reason, people think equines look like elk, I guess. A funny story I heard, but sad too, was about a hunting party that rode out on their animals into the Cascade Mountains. They secured their mounts to trees while they took off on foot. After a long day, one of the men finally spotted an elk and took aim. The animal dropped when shot. Excitedly the small group hiked to the area where the elk had been seen, and found…yes…his horse. He accidentally shot his own horse, and the others had broken free in sheer panic and scattered!

Many people ride alone. I often did this when I lived in Oregon. I'd ridden my horse for close to 20 years, so I felt pretty confident. However, in retrospect I realize it's not the best idea to ride alone. Occasionally someone is found dead because they fell off their mount for whatever reason and there was no one there to help. If you do ride alone, do yourself a favor and leave a note or tell someone where you're planning to ride and when you think you'll be back. Cellular service is pretty good nowadays, but not in all areas, especially remote ones. A few lone riders I know carry a device that alerts a search and rescue team…assuming there's satellite coverage. By all means, absolutely learn to use a compass and/or a GPS if you ride alone. Don't think compass knowledge is unnecessary. A GPS requires batteries…batteries die. Sometimes a GPS won't pick up signals if in heavy timber growth.

If you're riding in a group, make sure someone POSITIVELY knows where the group is going and how to return! Take your own GPS too. This seems like a common sense idea, but all too often it's not. However, if you do end up lost, you'll be happy you have your saddlebag with extra water and a snack bar or two, along with a lighter or matches to start a fire. Did you happen to pack a sweatshirt or jacket? You'll be glad you did.

It may happen at some point that your mule "escapes." I hope you're not like me. I have a tendency to go in one gate, mess around cleaning pens or filling troughs, then go out another to feed chickens, and I completely forget about the first entry. Should you discover your mule missing, get a bucket of grain and her lead line and rope. If you live near anyone with horses, check there first. I know exactly where Reba heads when she gets loose.

However, if you live in the country, the problem is much more complex and worrisome. I don't have an easy answer, but try to think like your mule. What would she be drawn to? Most likely food and companionship. Learn to lock the gate when you enter the pen, even if you turn around and leave through that same gate. Make it a habit!

My husband and I have always been trail riders, not arena folk. We've ridden extensively in the Cascade Mountain Range in Oregon, the Sisters Wilderness, and the deserts of Arizona. We've crossed rivers and bridges, climbed mountains and descended into canyons. We've made mistakes, some serious, but seldom the same one twice. Dangers aside, trail riding is a wonderful way to spend time with your animal and friends. The view from your saddle is magnificent, and the more you ride your mule, the more you'll come to know and trust each other.

Reba and Becky

Photo by Tom Coffield

Don't try to win over the haters: you are not a jackass whisperer.

Brene Brown

6. Problems

I once read that "there are no problem horses, only problem riders." You know what? I really wanted to believe this, but it seems overly simplified. While it is true that a rider can do many things that can cause problems for a mule (or horse), the fact is animals can have serious issues independent of human treatment.

Unfortunately, animal abuse is all too common. People starve and beat horses (and mules) sometimes to death. So, when you buy your mule, let's assume you're buying an animal that hasn't had abusive owners, has not been starved, punched in the head, whipped, or mistreated. However, an animal can have back, knee or other joint issues that cause problems, or perhaps it simply inherited a testy, nervous, high-strung disposition.

Remember that many seasoned riders consider a mule's disposition to be of major importance, if not the most vital factor, when buying one.

As stated before, probably the biggest issue a person can have with a mule is the mule's refusal to do something the rider may want it to do. For starters, you are not going to be able to force a mule to do anything it doesn't want to do. A mule cannot be beaten into submission the way a horse can. You need to use "psychology" on your mule, and even then that may not work. Mules do not forget…and they do not forgive. Most often a mule will get even if mistreated. Remember that. A mule will not do anything if it thinks it is going to be hurt by doing it. This is a good thing, really. You don't have to worry about the mule doing something stupid or dangerous, like jumping off a cliff into a steep gorge – at least I've never seen or heard of one doing that. If a mule firmly refuses to go down a trail, there's usually a really good reason!

So, what causes mule problems? Well, sometimes your mule will simply have an opinion that differs from your opinion. This is not a major problem. Try to see it from the mule's perspective. Is there something there that the mule thinks will "get" it? Take it easy, wait a few moments while the mule looks things over, then use your leg cues and urge the mule go the direction you want. If that mule continues to adamantly refuse, maybe you should listen, especially if this is a mule who typically doesn't do this kind of thing. An experienced rider could probably work through this refusal more easily than a novice, however.

I once had an episode when I was still riding my horse that taught me a good lesson: I was riding by myself into a canyon where I'd ridden many, many times, but that particular day my horse refused to go down the hill. I tried every maneuver I could and finally gave up. I began to worry that one of us was going to be injured in our altercation, and I strongly suspected it wouldn't be my 1200-pound horse. So, instead of trying to win the battle, I turned him toward home but went a circuitous route so he wouldn't think he could throw a fit and get to go home. As it turned out, I later found out there had been a bear in the canyon in that very area that morning. Another time this same horse refused to go down a trail back behind our house – a trail we'd traveled many, many times. Finally I decided to just take a different route. It was later that I discovered a cougar had moved into that territory. My horse also refused to pass by a bush on one of the rides I'd taken many times before. I kept nudging him on. Finally I stopped nudging and was sitting there thinking about the best course of action to take regarding this behavior. It was then that I noticed this continues noise.

At first I thought it was a cicada coming from nearby shrubbery, but when I looked closer I saw a huge rattlesnake lurking in the bush. We went a different way.

Mules (and horses) have far keener olfactory senses than people. They can smell things that people can't. They can hear things people can't. And the mule can see things a person can't see because mules can see behind themselves due to the way their eyes are set. So it's worth considering when your mule balks at doing what's asked of her, that perhaps she can sense danger that you have no idea is lurking. This is why riding in windy conditions can be a bit trying. Smells travel!

If you are a heavy-handed, demanding person, a mule might not be a good match-up. Conversely, if you don't give your mule proper guidance and leadership that makes her feel safe with you, other problems will arise. You don't want your mule to be the boss and take control. Your mule needs to respect and *trust* you. This has been an issue for me because I tend to be a bit easy-going and let things slide, especially if I think it's "no big deal."

Your mule may startle. Sometimes she may just stop abruptly, ears up, and stand totally rigid studying some object in the distance that has startled her. Sometimes your mule may spin about so quickly you literally won't even know what happened and she'll take off like the devil himself is chasing her. Mules are excellent at this.

Hopefully your saddle is set and you are not in la-la land when this occurs. Horses do this too, so don't think it's just a "mule thing," but my experience is that horses are not anywhere near as quick as mules at pulling this maneuver.

The first time Bucket spun about, dumped me, and took off, I was adjusting my reins and had let her start walking out. I wasn't paying the least bit of attention. Suddenly, I was on the ground before I even knew I was out of the saddle. To this day I have no idea why she spun about and took off. Fortunately, we had just closed a gate so she didn't go far. To be honest, my feelings were really hurt. My rear-end ached a bit too, but I was so stunned that she would do this to me after all we'd been through that I broke down and cried. Had there been something there that I could see that scared her, it wouldn't have been so bad, but there was nothing...nothing that I could see, hear or smell. Obviously, there was something there that Bucket could, though. Anyway, I mounted up and rode back to camp, but I felt devastated and betrayed.

With Reba, however, the entire episode was my fault. I was, as usual, in la-la land riding along thinking about who-knows-what. I watched my husband's mule (Levi) startle and start to spin because a "killer" rabbit unexpectedly jumped out of a bush right in front of him. I was chortling and trying not to laugh out loud, because

Levi is always Mr. Perfect. Tom stopped him instantly. Seconds later, as though an afterthought, Reba decided that maybe she should be scared too. She did a half-spin and took off. Unfortunately, I had not cinched up enough and my saddle went sideways with me in it. I had too much rein out to "whoa" her, so I watched the cactus and brush pass by my head as I clung to the saddle that sat on her sideways. She didn't lope far, and when she stopped by a creosote bush I decided that would be a good place to land since I couldn't pull myself and the saddle upright, and the bush had no thorns – one of the few thornless bushes in the desert! Well, for the rest of the ride I had to listen to my husband lecture me about cinching up, having less rein dangling, and paying attention.

Neither one of these incidents was because the mule was a problem mule. In both instances, *I would have stayed in the saddle had I been more attentive!*

Another issue that can arise, is that some mules (horses too) are prone to want to run up and down short inclines or passages. Do not allow this. It's a bad habit, and if there are other riders behind you they won't appreciate this at all because it may cause their mount to do the same. People get crabby about this.

Reba still does this from time to time...almost like she's testing me. I've tried several things to stop this behavior, but what works the best is if I take the time to turn her around at the bottom of the decline or hill and then ride her back to the top. Once there I make her pause a moment, then let her go down once again. Invariably she walks like she should have the first time. Weeks go by and then she tests me again.

Mules can be kickers. They do not like having their hind-ends crowded. So, if you're on a group ride, do not let the horse behind you crowd your mule. Mule riders are pretty good about not crowding the animal in front of them. Kickers can do considerable damage to stall walls, fences, other animals and people too, for that matter.

Some mules *(not all)* don't like small creatures in their pen or near them. This would include dogs and, unfortunately, sometimes little children. My husband's mule is one such critter. He stepped on our puppy when she ventured into his corral, and to this day he threatens to chase her if she comes too close. He even chases the chickens out of his pen. It seems this behavior stems from fear of being prey – or maybe it's just a territorial matter.

Mules do, however, yearn for companionship. They are a herd animal. Don't think you can buy one and keep it by itself. However, you don't necessarily need another mule as a companion. Mules tend to like horses, but they can become friends with other animals too, even dogs and cats. I have read that they prefer horses to donkeys. I know my Reba is absolutely crazy about horses.

Mules do better being fed in their own corral or pen and not being fed with another animal. Food was a big source of the squabbles that used to erupt between Levi and Reba. Even giving snacks when the mules are together can cause ears to go back, teeth to bare, and tempers to flare.

There is a lot of discussion about how much a mule should be fed. Some advocate that mules don't need to eat as much as horses – this is not necessarily true. I actually weigh Reba's feed because she is an "easy keeper" and I chronically tend to overfeed because I worry that the hefty gal might be hungry. Normally I feed her between four and five pounds of good hay twice a day. My husband's mule is served between five and six pounds of hay. Reba is also quite content to graze on shrubbery, weeds, limbs and such, while Levi very seldom eats anything but hay and, of course, treats we hand out.

Unless you grow your own hay, you'll find it expensive to buy nowadays. (And growing it costs money too.) Weighing it prevents wastage. I purchased a postage type scale on Amazon for about $29.00. I put the feed in a basket and weigh it that way. I feed more in colder weather. If you do this, be sure to weigh the empty basket first, then you'll know the exact weight of the hay.

Mules can have physical problems even though they are touted to be "ailment free." In fact, mules can, and do, colic. The saddest thing about this, is that because mules are so stoic, often you don't know there's a problem until it's too late. It's absolutely devastating and heart-breaking to lose any equine like this.

Mules can develop thrush, white-line disease, ringbone, and many other of the same ailments that horses can. I do think they just tend to get these issues less often, so overall they are reputed to be hardier than horses.

Teeth. If you've owned a horse, you undoubtedly know that teeth must be tended to because they "erupt" or appear to grow. Usually a vet takes a file and smooths out the sharp edges. This should be done yearly or bi-yearly. However, mules (and horses) might need more dental care than people realize. This is where a *certified, licensed equine dentist* is critically important. Do not allow anyone but a CERTIFIED, LICENSED equine dentist, or a veterinarian, to work on your animal's teeth. Would you go to someone for dental work who wasn't certified and licensed?

I wasn't aware of the importance of this until my husband's mule developed some very long lower "canine" teeth. The vet didn't have the proper tool to cut them back, so we took the mules to a *certified, licensed* equine dentist. (I only took Reba because Levi doesn't want to load without a friend in the trailer.) Our vet was there to sedate the mules and horses that had appointments that day. The dentist fixed Levi's problem plus a few others we didn't know about. I hadn't planned on letting her work on Reba, but since I was there I figured why not.

Much to my shock, Reba had some serious issues in her mouth! This quickly explained why she'd been in the habit of shaking her bit and in general messing around with it. The back teeth were shaped like a ski slope, forcing the teeth directly above to start impacting, which caused the teeth next to them to do such and such etc. I was stunned. The vet was stunned. These were things that were not visible without the apparatus to open her mouth wide enough to actually be able to see and feel the back teeth.

We brought the mules home, and the very next day when we rode I noticed that Reba no longer fussed with the bit and shook her head. Unbelievable. I felt the $135 fee for work on her mouth was absolutely worthwhile. So, it might be worth at least one trip with your mule (or horse) to a certified, licensed equine dentist to have their teeth checked out. If your mule's teeth need attention, it can cause eating problems and also behavioral problems when you're riding.

Finally, like people, mules have their own personalities and dispositions. Some are just naturally docile and easy-going while others are anxious. Some are lazy; others are high-strung. Some are terrific arena and show animals, a great many are excellent trail and pack animals, and it seems most like to have a job. And some are quite the pranksters and entertainers. I think mules tend to be calmer than horses and not as easily excitable or flighty. They can and do get mad, however. Remember that a mule does not forget...or forgive. They will get even! Be very judicious with any discipline. They seem to know if it's warranted or not.

I think that with time and a lot of attention, most mules bond with their owners and are *extremely* loving, wonderful companions.

7. Worms, Vaccines, Trailers and Such

"To worm, or not to worm? That is the question." Or wait, maybe it's "To vaccinate, or not to vaccinate?" These two topics, worming and vaccinations, produce myriad responses from mule owners. Everyone has an opinion, and you'll no doubt formulate one for yourself.

There are those who do not worm their mules, or who worm them sporadically at best. Others worm their mules on a regular schedule. Where and how your mule is kept will likely help you formulate an answer.

First of all, your veterinarian's advice should be heeded. No argument. Nowadays the tendency is to worm animals less often than previously recommended. This is either because the worms have become unresponsive to the medication, or because the animal just doesn't need to be wormed that often.

Beginner's Guide to Owning a Mule

If your mule will be on a pasture with a lot of other animals, it's probably a wise idea to have a regular worming schedule. If your animal is kept at home in its own pen or turnout, regular worming (meaning five times a year) may not be necessary. Once or twice a year may suffice. Your vet will know. You can also have your mule's manure examined for worms periodically to see if worming is needed.

As for vaccinations, this is another area where most everyone has a pretty strong opinion. I have our mules vaccinated yearly for West Nile + 3 Way and also rabies. Rabies is one of my personal dreaded diseases, and equines can get this deadly virus just as easily as any other animal. (I used to get our cows vaccinated for rabies too.) I do not have the mules vaccinated with the fall flu shot. I don't get the flu shot either. Our animals are not in a boarding facility or around large numbers of animals where they could theoretically pick up a virus more easily.

If you take your animals on large group rides often, or if your mule is in a boarding facility, you might want to consider getting more vaccinations. However, there are many people who absolutely do not believe it necessary to ever vaccinate a mule. Their thinking is that mules have that hybrid superiority and are less prone to illnesses than horses. And of course, many people nowadays question the need for vaccinations for anyone at all. I do highly recommend that you abide by your veterinarian's recommendations, however.

Supplements are another area of strong opinion. Again, your vet will be your best source of information and guidance on this. If you are feeding your mule quality hay, your mule probably doesn't need supplements.

I do give our mules a serving of Safe Choice Original Feed when I give them their monthly psyllium. I mix the two scoops of psyllium with a large yogurt container of Safe Choice in a bucket. I do this for seven days every month. They can't eat it fast enough!!

Finally, there's the issue of trailering, and this can be a monstrous issue. Hopefully your mule has been trained to load in a trailer when you buy her. Beware if the seller says he will deliver the animal…guess what that can mean? It can well mean that getting the mule into a trailer is an ORDEAL.

As mentioned before, many people say that mules generally don't like trailering alone. Reba loads alone very easily. Levi does not want to load unless there's another mule in the trailer. He *seriously* does not want to load. This is not a problem for us because my husband doesn't take Levi off by himself. I tend to ride with friends a bit more, so I'm happy that Reba doesn't hesitate to hop onboard. Bucket also loaded, but she wasn't a relaxed traveler by herself.

Verify with the seller that your mule loads without a civil war ensuing. It is extremely, *extremely* difficult to not teach an animal bad behavior or habits in trying to force them to load into a trailer. Many people try butt-roping. We ultimately resorted to this tactic probably half a dozen times or more with my husband's horse before he cooperated. Once he got the hang of it, though, he literally jumped into the trailer. You can also link arms with someone and kind of "walk" the mule into the trailer that way. Be very careful. This works with horses…I'm not so sure about mules and I hesitate to even mention it.

Some people advocate putting the animal's feed in the trailer so they have to enter to eat. The idea is that they'll get used to being in the trailer. This didn't work well for us because Tom's horse would grab a mouthful of food then soundly smack his head into the trailer roof removing scalp in the process of scrambling back out as though a boogeyman appeared . Some people try to entice the animal with treats like carrots or cookies. Others do the pebble toss…get a lawn chair, tie the mule up to the inside back of the trailer, and toss little pebbles at the mule's hind-end until he gets so annoyed he enters. This is definitely not a good technique, but it shows the desperation that some folks reach. Once in a while my horse would go on strike about loading. I have absolutely no idea why. All I had to do was get out the riding crop and show it to him, then walk behind him. He loaded right up. I never once had to tap him with it.

I don't have a magic answer for getting your mule to load in a trailer. I would suggest consulting a trainer or someone who really knows his/her stuff. Don't get hurt trying to load an uncooperative mule, and don't get your so mule riled up that loading becomes a future issue. If you put another animal in the trailer, it's very possible that, given her sweet time, your mule may decide on her own to load. Remember, you can't rush, or force, a mule!

As for trailers – these are expensive items, even the used ones, but if you want to ride in other locales, they're necessary. Many riders have two trailers.

One trailer we have is named "Plain Jane" for obvious reasons, and it's our official Mule Motel. It's a three-mule slant with living quarters. This is a luxury (to me) when we're out for several days riding. I have to confess that I don't do well in a tent. This is a trailer I don't like taking out for just a day ride, though. Often the roads on these shorter forays are extremely rough, bumpy, and dusty, and the inside of the trailer mysteriously attracts immense clouds of dust. The interior can look like a catastrophe struck if everything isn't securely stowed, not to mention that some trailheads just can't accommodate the larger, live-in trailers.

Our other trailer is a two-mule bumper pull that has a fantastic, spacious tack room and plenty of room (and head room) for two large mules. I really like this little one.

But people carry stock in all kinds of trailers. What you end up with will depend largely on the weather where you live and your budget. Just make sure the trailer has plenty of ventilation available. Animals can develop serious respiratory issues in trailers without adequate ventilation.

Keep your trailer clean. Remove all manure after *every* use. Rinse off all urine. Check the floorboards under the mats regularly! This is critical. Check your tires regularly. There's nothing quite like dealing with a flat tire on a trailer loaded with animals. I once had a blow out in the Mojave Desert. I was driving a small Class C motorhome with two dogs and a cat onboard and hauling a trailer with two horses. The motorhome's inside dually blew apart from road and exhaust heat. It was 120 degrees, and no one would stop! In fact, police cars drove by even though I put the hood up and flapped my arms like a lost pelican trying to take off. And guess what? AAA said I wasn't covered for hauling a trailer.

Finally, before my cell phone died, I got the number of a person who agreed to come out and help me change the inside dually, but even he couldn't do it. I ended up having to drive ever so slowly into Las Vegas to a tire shop where they told me it would be at least four hours before they could get to me. I begged the grumpy man to change the tire sooner, but he didn't care that I had livestock in a trailer in 120 degree heat. About that time my horse urinated, and it ran like a river across the parking lot. He changed his mind.

The point is, the tires were good, and the trailer tires were good. But the astronomically scorching road conditions, along with the motorhome exhaust, ended the inside dually tire. Things like this can happen.

At the end of the day, I had to bury the cat (Candy) in a dumpster at the rodeo grounds in Las Vegas where I stayed because she died of heat stroke and dehydration. I covered her nicely with a tablecloth and felt awful about where I was leaving her. I still feel really bad about that.

However, moving on...here's a way to have some fun with your mule and maybe ride a little more often.

It seems when people work full time, by the time they get home and prepare dinner and eat, the evening is shot for going for a ride (unless it's summer and still daylight). And sometimes the weekends fill up with kids' activities or other commitments. Before long, it may seem like you are riding only once a week and often not even that.

A possible solution to this dilemma is to construct a small arena. Don't panic. This is easy to do and not as expensive as you may think. The arena doesn't have to be a roping arena the size one sees at the rodeo grounds. A "loping" arena can meet your needs perfectly.

Our "loping arena" is approximately 75 x 65. We built it in about three days or so, but we do have warm weather that helps move things along. We dug holes and poured concrete, then we set the steel posts in. After they set-up, my husband then welded the top rail on, and he also welded loops on the posts that we ran wire through instead of adding steel rails (this saved a lot of money and works great). I had two loads of arena sand delivered which we spread. Overall, we spent about $900 for the steel, concrete, and wire. The arena sand ended up costing about $200 delivered.

Having something like this may well enable you to ride in the evenings, or to take a short ride at any time. I ordered a book from Amazon called *Western Practice Lessons.* It helps having something specific to work on with your mule rather than just trotting around in circles. That gets boring.

Just being able to saddle up without having to have another rider with me made a big difference in my confidence in riding my mule when I first brought her home. I also now have a great area to work on groundwork, too.

The same type of thing can be achieved with fence panels. The panels run about $100+ each, though…you don't get a very big arena for $1200 using fence panels.

Having this arena could add to your property value also should you decide to sell your home.

The gate to Reba's Arena

You've got to have smelled a lot of mule manure before you
can sing like a hillbilly.

Hank Williams

8. A Few Thoughts About Boarding

This seems like a self-explanatory, no-brainer topic, but I
have seen people leave their mule (or horse) in horrible
places, not really giving it much thought, searching only
for the least expensive, most convenient place possible.
For starters, if you cannot care for your mule yourself,
perhaps you might want to rethink whether you should
buy one or not. Boarding an animal is like paying
moorage fees for a boat. If you use the boat a lot, the fee
may not be so objectionable. But if you seldom have the
time to use your boat, the cost can become aggravating.
And as the boat sits unused, small things start going
wrong. The same applies to boarding an equine. If you
visit your animal and ride frequently, the boarding fees
might not seem so burdensome. If you leave your animal

in a facility for weeks at a time and don't ride, however, the expense will begin to enter your mind, plus it is a terrible thing to do to your mule, especially if the mule is kept in a stall most of the time. Dreadful.

It's very difficult for me to leave Reba and Levi for two to three months in the summer when we head north with our tugboat to work. I hate doing so, but my mule can't go with me!

So, if you must board your mule, full-time or part-time, here are a few items to consider.

First, remember that it will be a rare person who will care for your mule as well as you do. Your mule will be fed twice a day most likely. If you're very lucky the water in the trough will be kept clean. If you're *really* very lucky the pen will actually be cleaned twice a day – but usually only once a day. The manure may be picked up, but will your mule be left standing in urine soaked shavings or other ground cover?

This sounds dismal, and it's only the beginning. However, let me hasten to add that there are facilities that will take excellent care of your mule, but they will cost more – perhaps a great deal more.

So, where to start? First, get recommendations from other equine owners. Visit the facility long before you think about putting your mule there. Visit it several times…unannounced.

Boarding

1. Are the stalls clean? How often are they cleaned?
2. If animals are kept inside, is the facility well ventilated?
3. If animals are outside, do they have adequate shade/shelter?
4. Are the water troughs clean or are they filled with algae?
5. What kind of hay is fed? (You may need to take a few days to introduce your mule to a new kind of hay if your mule is fussy.) How often each day are animals fed? Is the feeding schedule consistent?
6. Will your farrier be allowed to come in and shoe or trim your mule? Or must you use their shoer?
7. If needed, will the caretakers put on and then remove a fly mask on your mule daily? Will they charge extra to do so? Fly masks should not be left on 24/7.
8. If you want special supplements fed, will they charge extra to do so? (You, of course, will have to provide the supplements.)
9. Will they spray for flies? (You will likely have to provide your own spray.)
10. Will your mule be turned out to self-exercise and run around? How often and for how long?

11. Is the facility a fire trap?
12. If the animals are kept outside or turned out, is the fencing adequate?
13. Are all equines required to have influenza and/or other vaccines appropriate for your area?
14. Are there restrictions on when you can enter the facility?
15. Finally, do the owners/managers seem genuine and trustworthy?

This is not an extensive list. There are many other items to consider. If the facility has an arena, are you allowed to ride in it? Do they give lessons? Be sure to clarify whether or not you want your mule ridden by anyone other than yourself!

Some facilities are absolutely top-notch and their fee will likely reflect this. Some clearly are not places where a responsible equine owner would want to leave their animal, but they are likely more affordable.

Even if you aren't boarding your mule full time, and you only need to leave your animal for short spells (for example if you go on vacation), don't be tempted to cut corners and leave your animal in a questionable stable. You could pay dearly in the long run, and vet bills can just be the start.

Another option for vacationers is to hire a house-sitter. We use to have a house-sitter who took our dog for walks and fed all the other animals as well (cat, chickens, mules). Our problem was that the lady didn't recognize bad hay (mildewed) which can show up once in a while. And, she was a bit frightened of the mules, so she didn't want to enter the corrals to scoop the manure. So then we had to hire a boy in the neighborhood to do that job. I will say, she loved our dog, though!

Several times we hired two "responsible" teenage girls in the neighborhood to come twice a day to feed the mules and scoop manure. We came home early one time to find several days' worth of manure not scooped.

A friend of ours hired a high school girl to feed her horses for a weekend while she was gone. She came home to find the horses without food and water. The girl "forgot."

Sometimes a neighbor (adult) can be helpful if you're gone for a short time. We use to have wonderful neighbors who were willing to feed for us when we were gone, and we did likewise for them.

It can be difficult (and expensive) to have animals and be gone for very long. The bigger the animal, the more the difficulty! Nowadays, when we leave for weeks on end in the summer, I take our mules to a place that's *almost* perfect. They mules have plenty of acreage to run free. They're never kept in pens. I provide the hay, so they are well fed. The woman is great about keeping troughs filled and clean. The shade/shelter available is definitely not what I'd like, but until I find some place better, this will have to suffice.

The woman really enjoys Reba and Levi, and she has three beautiful horses of her own. It's good for the animals to mingle which she allows after the mules and horses become friends "over the fence" for a few weeks. I leave treats for the mules with her, plus our veterinarian's phone number in case of emergency, and our farrier's contact number in case a mule loses a shoe. I leave extra fly masks in the event one gets mangled by mule play, and I make sure I leave fly spray also. I pay her at least half the fee up front in case she has unexpected costs come up for the mules. I call her periodically to see how things are going, and I make sure she has our contact number on the boat. I pre-pay our farrier also.

We have left our mules with others in the area, and I feel that the animals have always been at least adequately well cared for. When we started leaving for long periods, however, I needed more than "adequate care." My preference for where I keep them now is because of the acreage they have all to themselves to run around on. I can leave town and almost, *almost,* not fret about leaving the mules behind.

Boarding

When we pick the mules up, they seem very content. Levi is more anxious to come home than Reba, but overall the mules don't appear to be traumatized in any way. If anything, they've been a bit too well fed.

I once left my animals (horses then) with a person that I will never speak to again. Things seemed to be orderly and okay, but my horse's condition and reaction after being left convinced me otherwise. Thankfully the horses had only been left a few weeks, not months!

These are just a few items to consider if you find you must board your animal. Again, if money is no object, there are exemplary facilities, although it's not always easy to get into them. My friend left her dressage horse at a facility that not only groomed and saddled the animal for her before she came to ride, but they would also exercise the horse for her if she couldn't make it on any particular day. In addition, she took dressage lessons at the same place. Obviously she paid a great deal for these "benefits," but for her it was well worth it.

Boarding your animal may seem like a simple thing. After all, a lot of people do it. But proceed with caution.

She got too much fuel
She don't got a donk, this girl got a mule.

"Bunz" by New Boyz

9. Clinics: Life Changing

After many years of trail riding, I somehow got it in my head that maybe I should take a clinic. Imagine that! A number of people I knew spoke very highly about the Ty Evans Mulemanship Clinics, so when I saw that one was being offered not too far from my home and that several of my friends were going to take it, I signed up. I figured if nothing else it would be fun to get away and enjoy some mule friends for a bit.

Let me say at the start, my mule learned a lot at this clinic. I learned even more! As the clinic progressed, I couldn't believe I'd ridden for so many years and been so completely ignorant, and careless, about so many things. In fact, when I first started riding twenty-five years ago I knew no one who rode. I'd never owned a horse or been around horses. I bought an English saddle to use on a big quarter horse because I thought the saddles were cute, and so were the English riding outfits. You don't need to tell me how pathetic this is. I already know. Basically, I had no idea what I was doing. Somehow I survived. I had a pretty mellow quarter horse and a well-trained older Arab, and that's probably the only reason I'm here today!

So, right off there were three very important things I personally learned at Ty's clinic: one, how to control the animal's feet; two, small things matter; and three, I had to stop letting bad behavior slide on by. I have a tendency to be fairly easy-going when it comes to discipline (my two sons would not agree at all with this statement), so I have seldom made corrections in my animals' behavior. If it's a small matter, I tend to let it go thinking it's no big deal and it doesn't really matter. *It does matter.* This was only the tip of the iceberg, however. Every day the clinic was simply chock-full of friendly advice and instruction.

There were all levels of people and equines in my particular session (a few horses and a donkey were in the class also). Some people were relatively new to muledom, but most appeared to have done at least some riding, and at least one or two seemed like pros. Only a few mules and riders were quite green. I was surprised that several of the people had attended this same clinic before. After taking the class, however, I can understand why: there's just so much to absorb. Many of the people who were repeating also signed up for the advanced class scheduled for the afternoon.

The first day of Mulemanship 1, which was the level I signed up for, was a bit frustrating but *invaluable*. We spent the three hours doing groundwork. Technically, a person needs to be able to control the mule's feet to control the mule. Sounds simple, but I'd been curious how in the heck a person controls the feet. Well, I found out over the course of the three day clinic. But the clinic covered much more and, again, for me it was all about the little things: *asking* your mule for something and *getting* it…not letting it go if she doesn't respond appropriately; taking the time to correct her and not letting behavior slide, and not being so casual as to "not care if she does that – no big deal."

Many people reading this who have equines will be aghast that I had this laissez-faire attitude. It had served me just fine, however, *only* because of my exceptionally laidback quarter horse, and because my little Arab had been through 4-H schooling with his previous owner who was quite the young equestrian.

Anyway, on the first day we worked on a number of ground exercises. Reba did well on most of them, actually, except for one. When the instructor did the activity with her she performed perfectly, so it became pretty obvious that I was the one who needed the training!

We worked on half-circles (the difficult one for me), circles, engaging the hind quarters, and different techniques for backing the mule when on foot. Before I knew it, three hours had passed. We ended the class with a long question, comment, and answer session that was so informative.

Day two we saddled up, but we began by reviewing the groundwork from the day before. Then our first goal was to mount from a fence. This isn't all that hard (not falling off the fence was the hardest part for me). The other difficulty can be getting the mule lined up just like you want her. This is very helpful for people who can't mount from the ground.

We then learned to engage the hindquarters by learning a one-rein stop. This was all new to me! I seriously don't know where I'd been all the years I owned horses, but I obviously hadn't been in any clinics, that's for certain. We learned techniques for backing. Ty also showed us a method for bridling our animals. All too soon the morning session ended. We again ended the session with a group discussion and commentary. I regretted not signing up for the afternoon class also (Mulemanship 2) so I could continue working and riding.

The third morning we again saddled up and reviewed our groundwork exercises before mounting (either from the fence or a mounting block). This last day we worked on leg cues. We did numerous exercises like figure-8s and riding around obstacles using leg cues. We also learned about the three positions for changing speeds on a mule. This information seemed invaluable, like virtually everything else, and I started using these techniques the first ride I did upon my return home. Prior to this, I sometimes half wore myself out trying to get my mule to walk faster. Those days are over!

We again practiced the one-rein stop and backing and getting a "soft mouth." The class was so much fun that I hated to see it end. I had learned so much. I also readily understood that I had a lot more to learn!

I found it fascinating that not long after we began doing these exercises and activities, my mule began licking her lips, moving her mouth around, chewing on the bit, and in general giving every indication that she was seriously mulling things over – she was getting the idea of doing exactly what I was asking of her. She was likely also shocked that she was actually being asked to do something! One look at her face and a person could tell she was thinking and learning.

Now, despite all this training, catastrophe kind of struck when I decided I'd go on a group ride the second evening. This is actually very embarrassing to confess, but I'm doing this so if it happens to a person reading this book, they won't make my mistake...or feel like they're the only ones. Remember earlier when I talked about how overly excitable Reba became on group rides? Well, she reached a new peak.

Let's just say that Reba became *beyond extremely* excited when the ride started and had a *total* breakdown. I lost complete control of her and actually feared for my safety and the safety of other riders. It got even worse, however. I entered a fight or flight stage and utterly forgot all the things we'd learned about controlling feet...like circling her. Simple, but effective. After a mile of putting up with her nonsense of bucking, throwing her head and running out of control, I did the worst thing imaginable: I told the group I had to turn back, and I dismounted! Eeeks. Reba had become so unmanageable, however, that I truly feared for the safety of other riders as well as myself.

Well, if you know equines, you know that didn't go at all well. Once the herd of mules disappeared out of sight, Reba lost it and grew even more manic and intensely insane – if that's possible. I could barely hang onto her reins as she threw me around. I was tossed and shoved into bushes, jerked onto the ground, and nearly knocked over several times. No matter how many times I yelled "whoa" and "Stop it, you bitch," it continued unabated, and I seriously didn't know how much longer I could hold onto her. It took absolutely everything I had to keep hold of the reins. I knew if she broke free and ran after the other mules, someone would get hurt when she burst onto the scene in a mad frenzy. And then Kelly, a very experienced rider, came to my rescue. She hadn't felt right about my trying to leave on my own. *Thank, thank goodness!* Good lesson in that! I truly believe she prevented a disaster from occurring.

Within a few minutes Kelly managed to hook a rein to Reba's wildly tossing head and heaving body. I watched as Kelly jerked heavily on the rope halter and began to settle her just a bit. Still, Reba tried to run over the top of both of us. If I'd had a gun with me I might have ended it all right there. I hated that mule I had loved so dearly only hours before.

Kelly helped Reba gain control of herself after a few more tense minutes. I refused to mount up and said I'd just walk her back, so Kelly asked if she could ride my mule. I hesitantly consented, but only after I forewarned her and cautioned her to be CAREFUL. I wasn't able to ride Kelly's mule because that little critter had won a bronc bucking contest the year before and wasn't quite as safe and as settled as she needed to be; besides, I actually felt shaky and weak after my ordeal with Reba. So I walked Kelly's mule the mile back while she rode. Once back, I took charge of Reba and rode her for a good long while in the arena where she behaved like a civilized mule should!

Now, I seriously hesitated to share this awful story of my stupid behavior. I know better than to do what I did. It makes me look very bad, I agree. Again, I became more than scared and simply entered the fight or flight mode and could not think of anything except saving my neck. Staying on a big, wild, bucking mule just didn't seem like a good choice. Had someone been there to talk me through everything, I feel confident that I probably could have stayed on Reba and ridden through her meltdown. It would have been an invaluable experience for both of us.

There's another issue here, however. Reba has always behaved in a ridiculously excited manner when I've tried to do large group rides with her. This is the mule, by the way, that I was told did group rides just fine when I asked the seller about this. Well, I've come to realize that maybe she did do groups rides just fine when the mules were from the same ranch she lived on, and when there were only four or five of them going out, or even with a more talented rider. But it's a hard, cold fact that when she's riding with a large number of animals in a new area she gets "on the muscle" and wound up, although she *usually* settles down after 20 minutes or so.

I know there is really only one cure for this: I need to take her to new places and on group rides more often. You can see the catch-22 here: I don't want to do this because it's so unpleasant, but I need to do so to get beyond this. Reba behaves *very* well when it's just the two of us riding, which is what Tom and I do 98% of the time, so I know she can behave! She does okay with a small group – usually four or so. But beyond that, she can be a maniac. Surprisingly, or maybe not, it seems a lot of mules can have issues on large group rides. Could this be from not doing those kinds of rides often enough?

So, this is something to be aware of when buying a mule…there's group rides…and then there's "group" rides.

Since taking Ty Evans' invaluable Mulemanship 1 class, I feel more confident that I could handle a situation like this better the next time it happens – and I'm certain it will happen again, hopefully not as bad as this time. It's important to react sooner than later and not let the mule get so wound up. Circle and walk out of it. Circle the other way and walk out of it. Keep your seat. Heels down. I'd add that you need to remain calm which is pretty obvious, but that's a tall order when a person becomes fearful. I've been working on all of these things. Ty told us of one mule he had to circle over 250 times on one ride.

He said that by the end of the ride the mule made up its mind that it would behave much better next time out.

I learned good techniques at this clinic to practice with Reba that should give both of us more confidence in each other. I saw pretty darn good riders who left being even better riders after taking Ty's clinic. All of it takes practice and confidence. I'm doing much better at both.

So think about taking a clinic – it could change your life, and it will significantly improve your experience with your mule. As a bonus, you'll meet lots of great mule folks!

Advice from a Mule

Follow your path
Work hard
Pack life with great memories
Go slow and steady
It's okay to be a little stubborn
Get a kick out of life!

Your True Nature

Bibliography

There are many books about mulemanship and equines floating around. I have not read them all, and a few I read were disappointing. However, here are a few titles I can recommend.

Anderson, C.L. "Lee". *Developing the Art of Equine Communication.* Wickenburg, AZ. Moonlight Mesa Associates, Inc. 2012. (Not a mule book *per se* but extremely helpful in understanding equine behavior.

Foss, Jody. *Mules Across the Great Wide Open.* Mules Across America. 1995.

Hauer, John. *The Natural Superiority of Mules.* Guildford, CT. The Globe Pequot Press. 2005.

Hauer, John. *The Natural Superiority of Mules.* Second edition. Skyhorse Publishing. New York. 2014.

Jordan, Theresa J. PhD & De Michele, Peter E. M.Ed. *Overcoming the Fear of Riding.* New York. Breathrough Publications. 1996.   (Covers horses, showmanship issues, and fear of riding. Can be applied to mules.)